What Successful
Leadi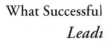

"*Leading Regular Folks* is a must read for anyone aspiring to a management position. Russ has drawn on his experiences in a variety of management positions to explain that you lead by example and with absolute integrity. He emphasizes that your greatest value as a manager is to manifest your talents through others, and that expectation levels drive results. This is an absolute blueprint to become a successful manager at all levels."

> —DAVID GLASS, Owner, Chairman, and CEO of the
> Kansas City Royals and former President and CEO
> of Walmart Stores, Inc.

"Russ truly captures the essence of leading the vast majority of organizational staff. His insights clearly define the skills needed to help people reach their potential and contribute to the overall success of any organization. As a CEO or President, I have been fortunate to lead for-profit and non-profit organizations in both Canada and the U.S. for many years. *Leading Regular Folks* is a must read for any manager or executive leader regardless of experience, as it reminds us of how we should be leading our teams and the people pathways to organizational results. I remain convinced that if we implement Russ's key leadership behaviors we will be recognized as the type of person for whom staff wish to work."

> —RICK BLICKSTEAD, President and CEO of the
> Canadian Diabetes Association and adjunct professor,
> University of Toronto

"*Leading Regular Folks* is the best book I have read that teaches principled, commonsense management. It would have been invaluable to me as governor responsible for 37,000 employees. From first-line supervisors to commissioners or CEOs, there is the need to be reminded that sensitive, practical teamwork pays off. Russ will help you achieve that."

— DON SUNDQUIST, Governor, State of Tennessee (1995-2003)

"Russ's leadership guidance should be made mandatory reading for every manager responsible for supervising and motivating employees. Calling on personal experiences, both good and bad, he describes the qualities necessary for a leader to inspire 'everyday folks' to achieve extraordinary results. You don't find these lessons in HR and business studies. This book is the leadership equivalent of *The One Minute Manager*."

— RON LOVELESS, former CEO, Sam's Club, retired, Walmart Stores, Inc.

LEADING
REGULAR
FOLKS

LEADING REGULAR FOLKS

What Matters Most in the Workplace

RUSS ROBERTSON

Leading Regular Folks LLC

LEADING REGULAR FOLKS
PUBLISHED BY LEADING REGULAR FOLKS LLC
Bentonville, Arkansas

ISBN 978-0-692-52276-9 (paperback)

Copyright © 2015 by Russ Robertson

Cover design by John Hamilton Design, Fort Collins, Colorado
Interior by Rose Yancik, Colorado Springs, Colorado

Published and printed in the United States of America.

2015—First Edition

10 9 8 7 6 5 4 3 2 1

Dedication

———

To my family and friends, the people who mean the most in my life. Especially to my wife, Sue, for your relentless dedication to things that matter most.

Contents

Introduction

There's a profound and universal truth about managing and leading that a great deal of individuals seem to not fully understand. The truth is this: *It is mostly about the people!* Contrary to what some might have you believe, good leadership is not rocket science. Nor does it require vast amounts of study to figure out that when you treat people with respect, help them feel like they're a meaningful part of a worthwhile endeavor, and inspire them in the right direction, the majority will give you a good effort. Many will reward you with their loyalty. And a *loyal* workforce that *willingly* puts forth a good effort is indispensable if you want your company or organization to excel.

Let's face it: Most frontline employees don't initially show up for work with the same mindset as the average manager or executive. Your company is likely made up mostly of what I call "regular folks," workers who join up with your organization because they need a paycheck. Initially, the number-one concern of most of the people on your payroll is not to make sure they are doing all they can to help your company achieve its financial goals and increase market share. Most won't be focused on helping to deliver products and services that surpass the competition until their leaders execute in a few key areas that will be discussed in *Leading Regular Folks.*

It's not that employees don't care about your company. It's just that at the start, what motivates and inspires them bears little resemblance to what drives the average leader in your organization. The keys to getting most regular folks motivated to do all they can to help your company achieve the overall goals is precisely what you will read about in the coming pages.

Successfully managing an operation of any kind that requires regular folks to get the work done is primarily a matter of how you communicate with people, how you make them feel about their role in the operation, and how you behave around them as their leader. Never underestimate the impact you have on the people you lead. How you lead and how you work with them carries an impact that can spell the difference between success and failure. Employees pay close attention to their leaders and they talk about you when you're not around.

Good leaders are on a perpetual quest for personal improvement. They have a clear understanding that the best shot they will ever have at reaching their full potential is to be concerned primarily with helping others reach *their* full potential. It's counterintuitive, I know, but the results are undeniable.

What you will read in *Leading Regular Folks* is not some trendy new management theory. The secrets you will find in this book come from the experiences of a person who spent nearly three decades leading and being led within a world-class, although not perfect, organization. Over that time, I saw the good, the bad, and the ugly (behaviors, not the movie).

I made leadership mistakes myself as I kept learning and

improving. I always wanted to be the best I could be. I had first-hand experience with some of the great business leaders of our time. One of them was Sam Walton. And for two different periods of time, I reported to a leader who was so well respected and admired he nearly had a cult following. I witnessed what can occur within an organization when people are led by individuals who have the ability to inspire rather than intimidate. And I witnessed firsthand some of the poorest individual leadership practices you can imagine. Those were by far the minority, but in some cases the results of their poor leadership impacted a lot of people, and not for the better.

This book is as much about those we lead as it is how we can excel as leaders. Without learning about followers we can't grow and improve as leaders. Further, this is not intended to be a comprehensive account of how to lead people or manage a business or enterprise. That would require a book so thick you wouldn't want to read it. I do not claim to be the world's foremost authority on leading people or managing a company. However, having spent the vast majority of my working life leading people within one of the most successful companies on the planet, I have gained unique insight into what I am convinced is the most critical aspect of leadership.

The number-one skill to learn, if you want to stand out as a leader, is the ability to understand what actually matters to regular folks in the workplace. You probably already know what matters most to you; now you should try to identify what matters most to those around you.

I know a lot about regular folks. I started out in business as one. And to this day, I have tried to maintain that outlook even after decades of serving within an incredibly successful company in a variety of hourly, managerial, and executive roles.

With that in mind, this book is a short training program in what matters most to everyday people who go to work, not necessarily because they want to, but because they have to in order to survive.

One other note. When I use examples of poor leadership in the chapters that follow, details such as time, place, and names have been left out in an effort to protect the identity of the persons involved. I made my share of mistakes, and it has never been my intent to hurt anyone or to make one person look good at another person's expense. If any of them should write a book in the future, I hope they would extend the same courtesy to me. Unless, of course, their portrayal is flattering. In that event, my given name is spelled with two S's and two L's.

Prior to sharing what took me twenty-nine years and four days to learn, I feel you should know a little more about me personally, as well as my background in business.

1

On-the-Job Training

Over a twenty-nine-year career, I and others like me received what may be the equivalent of a graduate-level education in business, management, personnel, and leadership. I reported directly to twenty-two individuals at different times. Many of these managers and executives would move up in the company, taking on more and more responsibility. One would rise to the position of vice-chairman, the number-two spot in the organization. Another would end up running the entire organization as president and CEO of our global company.

Additionally, I worked with and around a vast assortment of individuals who were charged with leadership at all levels and who came in all genders, shapes, sizes, and colors, and from nearly every background imaginable. Some were impressive and some were not. But one thing they all had in common was that they were expected to lead people in a manner that would consistently result in achieving our financial objectives and to one day help make our organization one of the best, if not *the* best, general-merchandise retailer known to man. It may sound overstated, but that was essentially our ultimate goal.

I realize that a large number of books on leadership, business, and related subjects have been written by professional writers and speakers who, in many cases, obtain their information not from the experience of leading in a competitive business environment, but from second- and thirdhand sources. There's nothing wrong with writing from that perspective or learning from those who do. But that is not what you will find in *Leading Regular Folks*. In this book, you will benefit from hard-won lessons and wisdom gained straight from the best teacher of all—years of firsthand, unfiltered experience.

It was through that experience that I learned the importance of something we oftentimes neglect to our peril. It's something many leaders forget as they move up. Or they simply fail to realize it until it's too late. The first lesson is: Who you are at the very core of your being is highly important to the people you lead. *Regular folks—the ones you are leading—are not impressed by your car, your home, or your expensive clothes. Your character and how you treat them personally is what matters most to them.*

You may feel you already have this figured out. If so, here is a quick way to find out, providing you are honest with yourself when answering these questions:

- Do you view your employees as a valuable asset or a renewable resource? (There are always more workers where these came from.)

- Do you tend to take yourself too seriously? (I'm the trained professional, the *real* key to making things work around here.)
- Deep down, do you feel that you're a little smarter, a little more important, and basically "better" than most of the folks around you? (I hold a master's degree from a respected business school, while many of the workers here barely made it through high school.)

If any (or all) of these resemble what goes through your mind when you think about your employees, you need to open your mind. In nearly three decades spent working my way up from entry-level sales clerk to regional vice-president and other executive positions with the world's largest corporation, I learned that good people, in fact, are not expendable. Nor is there an endless supply of them.

People add value to an organization not because they hold advanced degrees, drive an expensive car, or dress well. The most valuable people in your organization, the ones I'm calling "regular folks," bring value in ways that aren't determined by their home address or their mode of transportation for getting to and from work.

Your objective as a leader should be to learn about the regular folks in your organization and to refashion your approach to management so you can help unleash the tremendous resource that your employees represent.

Starting Small

I am the product of a small-town upbringing. I grew up in Rolla, Missouri, in a loving home with a mom and dad who have been married to each other since 1956. I have an older brother, Larry, and a younger brother, Mark. They are both successful in business.

I graduated from high school in 1978, and I have to say I enjoyed a Norman Rockwell childhood. I've been married to my first wife, Sue, for thirty-four years. We have two grown children: Tyler, who's married to Kate; and Brittany, who's married to Casey. (Casey is a man, by the way, a clarification that would not have been necessary back in Rolla during my youth.) So far, our children have given us two wonderful grandchildren!

While my work took us to five states over a twenty-nine-year career, Sue and I have now lived in the same house for twenty-two years. I have driven the same vehicle for thirteen years. I still have many of the same friends I've had since I was a boy.

I'm pretty steady in many of the key areas of life. Or perhaps I'm just boring. But either way, these are some of the things that make us who we are.

Learning to Lead While Doing a Job

I was in high school when I got an entry-level job at a small discount-store chain called Mohr-Value. This was the summer before my junior year. I went out and got a job because I wanted to buy a car. Since I wasn't getting paid to play basketball for the Rolla High School Bulldogs, the choice between sports and work was an easy one.

I began my career as a sales clerk in menswear, which in the old days required wearing a dress shirt and tie. I hated wearing a tie, and I took it off every time I thought no one was looking. My first day of work was June 26, 1976. I was sixteen years old.

About a year later, the company was purchased by a larger regional discounter that operated one hundred sixty-eight stores and went by the name Wal-Mart Discount City.[1] When I left twenty-eight years later, they were the largest company in the world, and, according to *Forbes* magazine, one of the most admired companies in America. This was true not because of me, and perhaps in spite of me.

For the final three-and-one-half years of my career, I held the post and responsibility of Vice-President of Career Development and Operational Training. I left Wal-Mart June 30, 2005.

In the years between my summer job as a sales clerk and my final post, I filled the roles of department manager, management trainee, assistant store manager, store manager, Sam's Club general manager, Sam's Club director of operations, director of the food-service division, director of sales promotion and marketing, regional manager, regional vice-president, and vice-president/divisional merchandise manager over general sporting goods. In every position I filled, I was learning on the job.

At one point in my career, I had the painful realization that I was not performing at the expected high level. As a result of learning from my mistakes while observing how regular folks responded to different leadership styles and behaviors, I improved on many of my shortcomings. This is not easy for any of us. Who wants it to be known that he or she is not measuring up in all areas of job performance? Most of us don't even want to admit that to ourselves. But being in these situations is how we learn, improve, and hone our skills as leaders. It takes a strategic commitment as well as a degree of humility.

Unlike the entertainment industry, my former company didn't spend a great deal of time recognizing ourselves for our vast achievements. We did, however, have a handful of annual inter-company accolades, and I was fortunate to be on the receiving end a time or two. I was honored and humbled. (In the interest of full disclosure, I was probably more honored than humbled.)

At the time I became a store manager, they told me I was the youngest store manager in the company. I also became the youngest general manager in our Sam's Club² Division (before my little brother became the youngest), as well as the youngest director of operations at Sam's. Some might say I peaked early.

Of the numerous performance reviews I received, most rated me somewhere above standard. One of the few times—if not the only time—I was rated outstanding overall was on a review written early in my career by a longtime family friend, Maxine Baird. (I will always be thankful for her early vote of confidence!)

While I usually was seen as being above standard by the folks charged with rating my performance, I did receive one below-standard rating. I could make an excuse for that one, but I won't. Part of being a leader is accepting responsibility for results, regardless of how you might perceive the circumstances. When your performance is reviewed and you are found wanting, it's time to commit to making the needed improvements.

From early on I had a desire to learn and grow from my mistakes, and I was open to change providing I didn't have to change who I was. Since we were all being paid to get results, I felt obligated to try my best, which included ongoing self-improvement.

I always was inspired by the good leaders as well as the poor ones. Leaders who consistently failed to treat people with respect gave me an inside look at who I *didn't* want to be. Over the years, I saw my share of managers and executives who fell into the "poor leader" category. They seemed to view our associates as a commodity rather than a human resource. I call leaders who don't treat folks right *BOONHAGS*, which is a coined word meaning "arrogant, self-absorbed, intentionally intimidating, and mean-spirited." I had no desire to be like them.

The business world is full of BOONHAGS, and seeing how regular folks responded to them gave me a strong motivation to never replicate their unsavory style and personal traits.

One particular BOONHAG who stands out in my memory was a guy who seemed to love watching folks sweat. As soon as he would walk into a store, he'd start acting as if it were his store and that the manager and all the other regular folks were only there to mess things up. He'd oftentimes say sarcastic and demeaning things that left folks feeling like he thought they were all a bunch of idiots and that he was the only person who actually knew anything. He rarely even spoke to the regular folks. It was as if he felt he was above communicating with anyone who wasn't at least a member of management. And as a bonus, he nearly always showed more interest in himself than he did anyone else.

The ironic thing was, he had started close to the bottom and had actually walked in their shoes. Typically, those were the leaders who had the best overall grasp of what actually matters to most regular folks regarding the people who lead them. But nearly every rule has an exception, and he was proof of that.

For all the time I spent observing leaders and assessing strengths and weaknesses, I was not a natural-born leader. Rather, I was someone who would have preferred to remain anonymously in the shadows. But Mac, one of my early store managers, explained that taking on more responsibility would affect the size of my bi-weekly paycheck. Since anonymous shadow work wasn't paying very well in the 1970s, I figured if I was ever going to be able to pay off my first car, I was going to have to do something other than stock shelves and point customers in the direction of the bathroom. Since I had no desire to spend one more day in a classroom then was required by Missouri law, I accepted the invitation to "go on the program" shortly after high school.

Initially, I wasn't interested in a career that left little time for extras such as sleeping. In those days, our store managers and assistant store managers worked six days a week—four long days and at least two very long days. My parents, however, encouraged me to give it a try. They said it was a good opportunity with a good company, which turned out to be good advice.

---

1. Since the inception of Walmart in 1962, the exact version of the company name has undergone several changes and updates. The current spelling of Walmart, which was in use at the time of this printing, will be used in the remainder of this book when Walmart is referenced.

2. Sam's Wholesale Club was the original name of what is now known as Sam's Club. The name Sam's Club, which was in use at the time of this printing, will be used in the remainder of this book.

2

Leaders Set the Tone

The overall expectation from those who supervised store-level management in the 1970s and 80s was lofty, to say the least. (Over time, I discovered the same high expectation existed throughout the organization.) Aside from working at least six days a week, store managers and assistant managers were expected to produce high-quality work while getting everything done as quickly and as cost-effectively as possible.

Like most publicly traded companies, we always were under expense pressure. As a result, being an assistant manager, in many ways, was like being an hourly store associate—but one who worked a lot more hours. We unloaded trucks, pushed two-wheelers loaded with merchandise around the store, stocked shelves, built merchandise displays, swept and mopped floors, and at times even ran a cash register. In short, we performed whatever duties were necessary to get the job done. In our spare time, we also did a little managing and supervising.

In those days, the executives who were charged with overall

responsibility for store operations and merchandise buying made most of the decisions that affected the stores and the employees. Input from most other home-office departments was limited primarily to the most critical issues. Store managers usually remained in good standing providing they consistently grew their stores' sales (top-line revenue generated from merchandise sales) as well as bottom-line profit, while keeping their stores reasonably neat, clean, and organized. You also were expected to maintain your merchandise layout according to the buyer-approved schematic known as "the modular."

A significant behind-the-scenes objective for store managers was to keep the home office out of your business as much as possible, especially personnel (HR), loss prevention (Asset Protection), and, of course, the legal department (Legal, Ethics, and Compliance). We also were expected to treat the associates right, which for a handful of wrongly focused store managers meant trying to keep their employees from contacting the district manager. Most of the leaders from district manager on up had little tolerance for a store manager who couldn't meet the basic expectations. We burned through a lot of folks in that role. Most of them left of their own accord once they realized this kind of work and/or lifestyle wasn't for them.

Although the company's principal leaders of that era were more than a little demanding, many were pretty forgiving. They seemed willing more times than not to give store managers a second or third chance, providing they hadn't committed some egregious violation of ethics, the law, or corporate policy. Sometimes, the second chance came after a manager had been fired. But still, a second chance is a second chance, regardless of the timing. Store managers who were terminated and eventually rehired would typically be brought back as assistant managers. Once they had again proven themselves, many were given an opportunity to manage another store.

Store managers in those days clearly understood that their primary focus was expected to be on generating sales revenue and profit while taking care of our customers and associates. We shared all sales and inventory information with the associates, along with the actual profit and loss statements (P&L). It was not uncommon for a store manager to copy the monthly P&L and post it in the break room. The statement detailed a store's financial performance for the previous month as well as year-to-date results. At one point in my former company's history, sharing this information on at least a monthly basis with all the regular folks was a corporate expectation.

With the exception of personnel records, the details of our business were an open book to everyone in the organization. It was obvious to most back then that Sam Walton believed there was power in sharing information and allowing everyone to feel a part of what we had going on. He believed that the more informed everyone was, the better equipped we all would be to implement practices that would translate into increased sales, greater cost-saving measures, improved customer service, and ultimately additional profit.

The result of such an open, informed environment was that you felt you belonged to something special. You also felt that you were a meaningful part of what was happening. Working there was more than just a bi-weekly paycheck. It was a shared experience and felt like a worthwhile cause to be a part of. All of us regular folks had as much opportunity as anyone to affect the results achieved by our store. And over the long term, the regular folks would benefit from the results.

In those days, operations management at all levels of the company understood that we had substantial room for experimentation when it had to do with finding ways to generate merchandise sales or reduce expenses. But we all knew when direction came out from any of our top leaders, it had better get done—and right away. That went double for anything sent out on Golden Rod, a yellow-paged memorandum that came directly from the home-office operations chief. It arrived on a company truck sealed in a blue company mail bag.

Every store manager knew that if you failed to execute the details of any direction sent on that yellow paper, you might not be the store manager much longer. In a sense, our condition of employment had a lot to do with our effectiveness at executing the details of those periodic Golden Rods. And beyond question, we knew what most of our executive leaders stood for, something I'll focus on in an upcoming chapter.

LEARNING THE HARD WAY

I recall the first time I was personally "made aware" of the importance of executing on home-office direction. It resulted in my having my business face blow-torched. (This was not highly unusual prior to the current era of kinder and gentler executive leadership.) The lesson I was treated to came at the hands of our district manager—known today at Walmart as market manager. Although this particular lesson came in the form of a group torching, it burned enough that I remember it vividly after thirty-five years.

It took place as a follow-up to a surprise store visit from a company executive who had a reputation for leaving behind him a trail of casualties whenever he toured stores. He came to our store for a walk-through, and when he left we went back to work, relieved we had survived the visit. Now here comes the leadership lesson.

The executive stopped back in our store the next day, which came as even more of a surprise. He made a quick run-through, checking to see what we had gotten done since he had given us his input twenty-four hours earlier.

We would quickly find out that we hadn't accomplished nearly enough.

Shortly after the executive left the store following his second visit in two days, our district manager showed up. He looked like he'd been in a fight with a pack of wild dogs and lost. He gathered the management team and, as they say, "tore us a new one." We were lit up for our collective lack of follow-through. He was right on target with his criticisms, and it made a lasting impression on at least one young, aspiring leader. Me.

Later that day, I watched our store manager walk out the front door, minus the huge ring of keys that previously had hung from his belt. (In the old days, you could tell who was in charge by who had the biggest set of keys.) He had been demoted, or in the vernacular of the day, "busted" to assistant manager.

Up to that point, I had worked in three stores. This was the second time I'd witnessed a store manager lose their job. It would not be the last, and I was beginning to get the picture.

In this particular situation, the manager wasn't demoted because of this one incident. He was removed from his responsibility because he had failed to create an atmosphere that resulted in his team consistently executing the details of the company program. And part of that program was responding with urgency when situations dictated.

He was a nice guy, and we all liked him. I recall feeling a sense of loss because he was a good person and had treated me well. But, like me at the time, he had yet to learn how important it was to establish clear expectations with those he led and to be respectfully relentless in following through on the execution of the expectations. From my view, his failure in that important area resulted in his job loss.

Later in my career, when I recalled all the managers and other leaders I'd seen demoted, the important lesson came through. *Getting results in any industry that involves people doesn't have as much to do with your knowledge, intelligence, or overall ability as it does your leadership. Specifically, it comes down to your effectiveness at accomplishing the most important things through the people you lead.*

Today, I can't begin to count the number of times I witnessed people at nearly every level lose their jobs because they hadn't learned the most important aspect of personal effectiveness. To achieve results as a leader, you need to know that your success has more to do with your relationship with the people you lead than any other single aspect of being in charge.

Your primary role as a leader, at whatever level you occupy, is to lead folks in a respectful, straightforward, and accountable manner. Holding people accountable has nothing to do with your being mean or acting tough—many leaders fail to understand this. Establishing expectations, and holding your employees to a level of performance that results in the achievement of those expectations, has to do with your expectation level of yourself as their leader. It also follows from the overall manner in which you interact with the people you lead.

If the expectation you set for yourself is to achieve consistent execution in your role by achieving the maximum feasible effort from those you lead, some of these principles will almost come to you naturally. These are the specific things we'll review as you read further.

3

Integrity Is
a Leadership Advantage

Everyone is born with one shot at earning a reputation that is above reproach. It requires a twenty-four-hour-a-day focus and takes an entire lifetime to achieve. When you occupy a position of leadership, the importance of your personal behavior cannot be overstated.

How you behave matters and it matters *all the time*, not just when people are watching. Leaders cannot afford a lapse in judgment when it comes to their personal behavior, and none of us deserves a pass because of our job title or tenure. Everything you do and say matters when you're responsible for leading people.

You might argue that who you *really* are is different from what others think of you. If that's the case, this bears repeating: *Perception is reality.* Here is a real-life example:

If you are married and one of your associates spots you dining out with someone who appears to be your spouse but isn't, you may have opened the door for speculation around the workplace regarding whether or not you are a devoted wife or husband. When you give people even the slightest reason to question your marital loyalty, it probably will not be long before they'll begin wondering about your loyalties to the people with whom you work. Even if you were having dinner with your sibling, the damage may already have been done. Remember, it only has to "look" like it is something that puts you in a bad light. If the perception is that you were dining out in an intimate atmosphere with someone other than your spouse, that perception is what will stick in the minds of those around you.

I won't take time to share how you might avoid perception problems on issues such as this one. Not allowing situations to take place that could result in a loss of respect from others is up to each of us to handle personally. No one else can earn you a good reputation.

To some, having dinner with a friend may seem like a ridiculous example. If you feel that way, ask yourself if you are being naïve—and whether that might come back to hurt your reputation. When most regular folks witness something that looks less than completely honorable, oftentimes they will assume it *is* less than honorable. They won't ask you for clarification, and they'll rarely take the time to investigate the details. And it is useless for you to argue against a person's reaching an inaccurate conclusion after seeing you in a situation like this with someone who isn't your spouse.

If a manager has an off day, for whatever reason, and allows that to affect the tone of how he or she talks to employees, the employees will not usually analyze why the manager might have been off his or her game today. Rather, they will begin to doubt whether their manager is someone who actually respects the people who work there.

Perception is reality, and it does no good to insist that is not the case. Let's say you put yourself in a situation that others perceive to be unethical or in some way less than aboveboard. Even if appearances are inaccurate and the situation in fact was ethical and completely aboveboard, it doesn't matter. The damage already has been done. Depending on the severity of what was suggested by appearances, you may have a difficult time recovering from your staff's low opinion of you.

You need to commit yourself, now, to always operate in every situation in a way that is above reproach. If, for example, you have ever shown up for work with alcohol on your breath, you should commit to never again allow that to occur. It doesn't matter that you were not under the influence. (The only exception to the required commitment in this example is if you are in charge of quality control for a company that brews beer, makes wine, or distills spirits.)

Most regular folks would not think poorly of you for consuming adult beverages in your off time. But when you show up for work with any sign that you are less than one-hundred percent ready to handle your responsibilities, you have put yourself in position to lose respect. Your associates may question how seriously you take your responsibility as their leader. In those kinds of situations, you set yourself up for a potential ding to your reputation. (And keep in mind that reputation is synonymous with integrity.)

You don't have to be a saint to develop a reputation as a person of strong character and integrity. But if you desire to be a leader who's known as a person of high integrity, conduct yourself overall in a manner that might earn you at least a runner-up in a contest for saints.

DON'T LOOK THE OTHER WAY

What you don't say can be as important as what you do say. Likewise, what you choose not to act on is just as important as the actions you take.

When you observe less than credible behavior in others but turn a blind eye, the effect is not much different from giving your approval. Let's say you are aware that a leader who falls within your area of influence routinely talks down to the regular folks. Or perhaps he or she even uses off-color language in their presence, but you don't take the needed action. In the eyes of the employees who are affected by that person, your silence is tacit approval. It is not much different from your instructing the leader to behave in a way that is disrespectful toward the regular folks.

As a leader, you're responsible not only for your own behavior, but also for the behavior of those you lead. It is up to you to not only set a good example, but also to respond appropriately when others violate your organization's code of moral and ethical conduct. You can't control someone else's behavior, but if they are unwilling to change once you have clearly established the expectation, you have a choice to make. Should that leader remain in their role or even in your employ?

Associates will rarely do their best work or give their best effort if they feel their leaders are anything less than completely honorable and trustworthy. And any establishment that doesn't have a reputation for absolute integrity throughout the entire organization is at a competitive disadvantage with industry peers that do. Who wants to do business with an individual, a company, or an association that gives you any reason to wonder about how honestly they conduct business? In such a situation, you would likely move your business to a competitor whose reputation is beyond question.

WHEN YOU MESS UP

We're human beings, and by our nature we have the capacity to mess up. No individual is immune from making mistakes, and none of us is guaranteed an unblemished future. But when we do mess up, there's one primary thing that separates those who have a chance to overcome it and those who don't. It's simple, but it's a difficult thing to do: Own up to your actions—all of your actions, including when you mess up in huge fashion. Don't believe the lie that if you just bluff your way through or somehow cover up the issue, it'll go away. It won't go away. And trying to hide what you did will multiply the penalties you will face and the scrutiny you will experience from those who work with and around you.

The truth is this (you might want to write this down). When you make a mistake, *nothing* will help you overcome it and move beyond it more effectively than taking these five steps:

1. Openly admit the facts of your actions. Don't sugarcoat it, don't try to justify it, and don't try to blame it on someone else. Admit what you did with no excuses and no spin.

2. Apologize to everyone who was affected by what you did.

3. Ask forgiveness from those who were harmed in any way by your actions.

4. Commit publicly that you will not allow a thing like this to happen again.

5. Do what is necessary in your life to ensure that you will, in fact, avoid making the same mistakes again. If needed, consider enlisting the support of a friend, mentor, or accountability partner. But do whatever it takes to make sure your future behavior in that area is the exact opposite from your past behavior.

FIVE-STEP RECOVERY PROCESS IN ACTION

I worked with an honest, talented, hardworking, respectful, and respected manager who was terminated for making an error in judgment. It came to light that he had done something that, in the world of law and order, would not have been even a misdemeanor. But within the boundaries of complete and total ethical leadership behavior, it was determined to be an action that justified, and called for, termination. It had to do with something he communicated in an email.

He is one of a small number of people whom I have known personally (or even read about) in business or politics who willingly and openly admitted his mistake. He apologized to everyone who was affected, as well as to many who were not directly affected. He also asked their forgiveness and committed that he would not do that or anything like that again.

He chose not to spin the details of his actions or blame anyone else. He had made an error in judgment and he didn't attempt to make an excuse.

When he told me what had happened, he said he was afraid I'd lose respect for him as a leader and as a friend. In reality, the high level of respect I already had for him increased to a degree. Today, I hold him in even higher regard. Owning up to his mistake and taking responsibility for his actions were two further signs that he was, in fact, a person of integrity. And although my friend is a very devoted husband and father, he didn't use the ubiquitous excuse that he was leaving his job to "spend more time with his family." He admitted openly that he had been terminated because he had messed up as a leader. Many would see him as someone to be admired.

Integrity has been described in many different ways. If you ask five people what integrity means, you would likely get at least five different definitions. To me, it looks like this:

> How I want my wife, my children, my grandchildren, and all the people who have known me best over the course of my life to view me on the day they put me in the ground. If you want to be remembered as a person who tried to always tell the truth, did what you said you were going to do, refused to cheat in order to win, treated others with respect and compassion, admitted when you were wrong and said you were sorry when you were, was faithful to your spouse and loyal to your family, appreciated your good friends, and tried to never forget where you came from, then you have to make the conscious decision to try to live your life every day in a manner that proves beyond question that that is in fact who you are.

With that in mind, you should give some thought to how you want to be remembered by all the regular folks you work with after you walk out their door for the last time.

I know the stories of an astounding number of managers and leaders who messed up and afterward handled it badly. Many never fully recovered. With few exceptions, the individuals involved chose to either spin the details of their behavior or to act like it hadn't happened. The inevitable result was they were not fully trusted, respected, or admired again by the people they formerly led.

They say your reputation is built slowly and over a long period of time, but lost in a moment. That is a cliché, but it's true.

So if you mess up, look your people in the eye and tell the truth. I guarantee they will respect you for it. They will also be willing and glad to line up behind you. And as a bonus, you won't put anyone in the uncomfortable position of having to lie at your funeral.

Here is truth that I don't want you to miss: *The only thing we have that can't be taken from us is our personal integrity. It can only be given away. Guard it like it's your most valuable possession.*

4

Take Responsibility
and Do Not Pass the Blame

When you are put into a new responsibility, don't act like you are still in your old one. If you get a promotion, a transfer, or any other shift in responsibility, don't hesitate before taking charge.

People who are given new responsibility, especially when that responsibility is over a business unit they are not familiar with, oftentimes don't initially know what to do. But those who take hold right from the word *go* are the people I admire. I don't know what separates those who hesitate from those who jump right in, but I do know the difference in the effect of one over the other. Leaders who not only accept responsibility but, without a second thought, *take* responsibility gain the respect and admiration of the folks around them. Regular folks appreciate a leader who takes charge and, when he or she makes the typical beginner's mistakes, doesn't try to dodge the blame. Rather, these new leaders stand up and take it like an honorable individual who's not intimidated by responsibility and the weight that it carries.

DON'T EXPECT A HONEYMOON

At my former company, any time you stepped into a new role there was not much of a honeymoon period. Every aspect associated with your new responsibility was on you the day you reported. This included the responsibility to start improving anything that was below standard before you got there. As the leader, you were expected to take charge immediately. If you hesitated or delayed, you would not be looked upon favorably by the leaders you reported to. Likewise, the regular folks who reported to you would begin wondering why you were chosen to be their new leader.

A great example of this occurred during a weekly merchandise meeting, which took place every Friday afternoon in our home-office auditorium. This meeting was attended by the officers who headed up buying and related activities for each of the merchandise categories and by the officers who were responsible for the supervision and overall operations of the stores. In one of these meetings, a regional vice-president asked what was being done to deal with a widespread overstock issue on a particular item. The person who was newly in charge of that merchandise group (for a total of four days) responded, "Well, first off, I inherited the problem." That response drew disapproval from nearly everyone present. The new head of the merchandising group in question was nearly booed out of the auditorium!

It's true that the problem that was raised had been an issue, and a widely known issue, for some time. But the new leader didn't receive a free pass just because he had only recently arrived in the job. I recall thinking that he *might* have gotten by with passing the buck had he been on the job only four hours. But he had been there four whole days. From the viewpoint of most of the people present, being in charge for that length of time left no room to invoke the "I just got here" excuse.

Take responsibility the minute you're put in charge. Regular folks will not respect you when you make excuses or blame others.

THE BEST TIMING IS *NOW*

That incident was a reminder that timing is also a key to just about everything in a world that involves people. When it comes to taking charge of things in your area of responsibility, your timing is rarely going to be off and you will rarely go wrong when you jump in right away and with both feet.

Too many managers and other assigned leaders handle responsibility as though they've spent most of their life learning the art of dodging and blaming. There's little doubt that passing the buck and assigning blame to the person who came before you comes naturally. It starts early when you get caught by your mom with your hand in the cookie jar. You automatically blame your little brother or sister. If you are an only child, you blame someone else's brother or sister.

But blaming someone else for what is lacking in your area of responsibility accomplishes nothing productive. It makes you look out of touch with your own business unit. And it may even call into question your character. Not accepting immediate responsibility for *everything* pertaining to your new role also gives people who are charged with evaluating your performance an immediate reason to question whether you are the right person for the job. Perhaps you are instead a person who wears the badge and maintains what was already there, without doing what it takes to make things better.

Large numbers of people have the ability to maintain what others created. But maintaining your area of responsibility without making improvements to move forward will result in your moving backward. If the competition is moving forward at a faster rate than you are moving forward, the effect is nothing short of moving in the opposite direction. In contrast, leaders who grab onto responsibility and never hesitate to take charge rarely stay where they are for long, unless they choose to.

The next time you are given a new area of responsibility, consider taking these three steps:

1. Prepare yourself mentally to take charge and accept responsibility the minute you show up in your new role. (Don't allow yourself to remain in the mindset of the previous role you filled.)

2. Commit that from the day you report you will not allow yourself to blame others for anything in your new area that's less than stellar.

3. If you feel the need to make someone aware of any problem in your new area that was left by the previous

manager, providing it was not a legal or ethical issue, share it with your dog. If you don't have a dog, share it with your neighbor's dog.

And when possible, avoid the temptation to share leftover issues with anyone at your place of employment. Remember, there is a huge difference between assuming responsibility and taking it. And this principle applies whether you're the lowest person on your organization's leadership totem pole or the president of the United States.

The next time you find yourself taking on new responsibilities, even if you are not real sure of what you are supposed to do or how you are supposed to do it, remember: Don't assume responsibility, **take it.** *Nearly everyone will respect you for doing so.*

5

Make Clear
What You Stand For

People do not enjoy working for individuals who continually change the rules or leave room for misinterpretation regarding what's most important. Simply put, your employees want to know what matters most to you. They want to know what you expect of them and, at minimum, what they can do to stay out of hot water. If you are consistent about communicating what matters most to you, your employees will nearly always try to meet the standard.

If you want your employees to be focused and motivated, devoting their best effort to the most important goals, it's up to you to relentlessly make known what matters most.

When you walk into a room full of your associates, what's the first thing that pops into the mind of each one regarding you? When they realize you're about to show up in their area of responsibility, what will they rush to attend to first? What is the one thing they would be most likely to break the world record in the one-hundred-meter dash to check on before you see it? Answer those questions and you will know what they think is most important to you.

In addition, the behavior your employees demonstrate toward one another as well as toward your customer is a good indication of the level of respect they hold for you as their leader.

How You React Proves the Importance

Regular folks also notice how you react to exceptions when you find them. Let's say you are in the business of selling stuff out of a building and you have established that having BOONHAG Bonnets on hand at all times is an absolute priority. Let's also say that you have explained why having the item in stock is critical to the overall success of your business, and you have made this clear to everyone who has influence over this item.

Now let's say you walk by the place where BOONHAG Bonnets are normally displayed and there are none. In the world of retail, that is called "out-of-stock" and it will have a negative effect on your bottom line. If your reaction to discovering there are no BOONHAG Bonnets for your customers to buy is anything less than what some folks might consider an overreaction, you have missed out on an opportunity to further convince your associates that you are very serious about being in-stock on BOONHAG Bonnets. And when you do react in a fashion that is respectful yet perhaps borderline insane, you will remove any doubt that being in-stock on BOONHAG Bonnets one-hundred percent of the time is without question an absolute expectation.

When you handle yourself in this manner regarding the things you feel are most important, it will not be long before everyone will know beyond question what you stand for. And it won't take long before they will place the same level of importance on your absolute priorities.

Employees also pay attention to how consistent you are in acknowledging those who execute on the priorities. If you call positive attention to those who execute on the things you feel are most critical to your business, it further establishes in the minds of employees what your absolute expectations are. Be clear and consistent.

Use a variety of ways to communicate the same priorities. And be careful to avoid sending a mixed message. Any ambiguity on your part leaves room for doubt, and that's the last thing you want. When you leave room for doubt, you can darn well bet your associates will do just that. They will doubt your focus as well as your commitment to your previously stated priorities.

If you want to succeed (and remember, your success is closely tied to the performance of your employees), you absolutely have to make clear—always and in many different ways—what you consider to be most important. Here is a simple exercise that will help you in this area:

1. Identify the top few (I suggest no more than five) opportunities, actions, or behaviors that you feel will have the greatest positive impact on your business or endeavor. Write them down.

2. Commit in your own mind that you will *never* accept less than excellence regarding these priorities.

3. Communicate your short list of critical priorities to everyone within your area of responsibility, starting with the individuals who report directly to you.

4. Going forward, stay relentlessly focused on every aspect involved with achieving excellence in each of the areas, and respond appropriately when it does and does not happen.

I used to report to a guy who far and away stood for "extremely" neat, clean, and straight. There was nothing he placed more emphasis on and there was absolutely no question that these three priorities were nearly sacred to this man. He insisted on cleanliness inside and outside our operating units, and he had a penchant for things being lined up neat and straight.

As a result of what nearly everyone believed he stood for, the people whose behavior he influenced spent a great deal of time and financial investment working on what they perceived to be his top priorities. They did this even though some questioned whether the difference between the normally accepted "reasonably" neat, clean, and straight and "extremely" neat, clean, and straight would have a positive impact on the profit-and-loss statement.

Another example was a leader I worked with named Hank. He nearly always devoted most of his efforts to improvements he felt would show up as gains on the profit-and-loss statement. He maintained a relentless focus on merchandise sales and on keeping expenses as low as possible.

Although I don't recall Hank winning a lot of awards for neat, clean, and straight, he routinely operated high-net-profit operations while staying within the parameters of what was typically acceptable regarding operational standards. Hank didn't get caught up in ancillary details. Rather, he stayed focused on things that would have the greatest impact on the income statement: sales, gross margin, and expenses. To his further credit, he did this while treating all the regular folks and customers with dignity and respect. Mr. Sam seemed to always appreciate leaders like Hank!

THE FOUNDER'S EXAMPLE

Perhaps the best example I've personally witnessed of someone who knew what they stood for in business was the founder of what would become the world's largest company. If you were to ask anyone who was ever around Sam Walton to name his top two business priorities, with few exceptions they would say something very close to "buying and selling merchandise and taking care of the customer."

Mr. Sam was so much about the merchandise and every detail that affected what we sold in the stores that the quickest way to mess up when he was in your store or area of responsibility was to begin a sentence without first pointing out what was selling. Or at a minimum, by mentioning something that directly impacted the top line (sales revenue). And as many of us experienced, he was not the most patient of individuals regarding failure to execute on the things that directly affected the top and bottom lines of your P&L.

When it came to customer service, or as he would often express it, taking care of the customer, he never left room for anyone to doubt where he stood on the subject. Everyone in the organization knew he expected us to stay focused on the people who shopped in the stores, always providing them with a positive experience. And the quickest way to draw negative attention to yourself from the man who invented Walmart (or from his top executives) was to mistreat a customer or an hourly associate.

If you think this is an exaggeration, ask any current or former company associate who ever had a one-on-one business conversation with Sam Walton or who spent time walking with him through company stores and warehouse clubs. He was so relentlessly focused on everything having to do with merchandise, along with the customers who bought it, that his passion for the business we were in flowed through to most of his associates. This was evidenced over a long time period by Walmart's consistent growth. His passion for the business we were in was so infectious that it even rubbed off on his father, Tom. The senior Walton, even in his nineties, routinely visited the three Walmart stores that were located in the town he lived in. He would come in to talk to us about the company, his two sons, and sometimes, to point out how we compared in price to the competition. On one of Tom Walton's approximate every-third-day visits to my Columbia, Missouri, store, he came in for the express purpose of making me aware of an item on which our number-one competitor across town was beating our price. That was embarrassing, and we tried hard to make sure it didn't happen again.

I'm convinced that Sam Walton's unbending focus on merchandise as well as the customers who shopped in his stores had nearly everything to do with my former company's rise from obscurity to the pinnacle of the Fortune 500. He took a concept that had been the basic business model in use by other companies and, once his stores built up a head of steam, seemingly blew past all of them as if they were standing still. His stores would not be undersold and we would try hard to always have the merchandise that people most wanted to buy. He was committed to the customer and preached merchandising to the management team.

Although I've never run across anyone who knew or worked around Sam Walton who doubted for a second whether he was one-hundred percent aboveboard, the first thing he nearly always talked about had to do with merchandise sales or the customer. And make no mistake about it: He left absolutely no room for anyone to doubt whether he expected the same focus and passion from all of us!

When you know what you stand for and consistently conduct yourself in a manner that never leaves room for anyone to wonder what you value most, the folks you have influence over will spend their time and your organization's money working on the right stuff. *Determine what you stand for and never leave room for anyone to doubt what it is.*

6

Prove You Are Interested in Those You Lead

I t matters to regular folks whether their leaders are interested in them not just as employees but also as individuals. The typical employee is just like you and me: He or she wants to feel they matter.

Employees are not inspired nearly as much by the corporation they work for as by the individuals they report to. The company matters, but individual leaders matter a lot more. It's easy to lose sight of this truth the farther you move away from living like a regular person. Getting promotions over the years and improving your own household cash flow can dull your memory of how most people view the world.

It can be hard to recall what it's like to be on a sales floor, on a loading dock, or standing all day behind a cash register. And if you have never held at least one job of this type in the industry you work in, or a similar job in any industry, it's more difficult to fully appreciate those who do. I'm not suggesting that if you have always been a banking executive that you can't possibly relate to the regular folks who are your clerks, tellers, and junior managers. But it has been my experience that if you want to understand the folks who interact with your customers and do most of the front-line work that drives your business, you'll have to make more of an effort in the direction of trying to understand what it might be like to have a job like theirs than a leader who *has* had a job like theirs.

If you are responsible for determining who will be put in charge of your individual business units, branches, or stores, never forget how important it is that those leaders have the proven ability to inspire regular folks. Sometimes you won't know for sure until you give a new manager a chance; and sometimes you have to take that risk. But when you get ready to make those important decisions, remember this old saying: The best predictor of future behavior is past behavior. Put another way, an uninspiring manager will not all of a sudden become an inspirational leader just because they receive a new title.

This is so important because if employees don't willingly get behind their immediate leader, it's highly unlikely they're going to be excited about lining up behind their company. How each employee feels about the company has a lot to do with how he or she feels about the on-site leaders. Sure, some employees will be interested in knowing about the people toward the top of the organization. But most regular folks aren't nearly as concerned about who's running the organization as they are the individuals who have day-to-day influence over them personally. As seen through the lens of most employees, their immediate leaders *are* the company. If you buy into that, make every possible effort to employ, develop, and promote individuals who understand that it's mostly about the people they lead. You will nearly always achieve better results with a leader who can inspire associates to perform at a higher level than one who simply demands performance. You cannot *make* employees give their best effort any more than you can *make* them feel proud of the organization that employs them. Leaders who show a sincere interest in the people they lead are far more likely to get top performance from their employees. It's not necessary to know every detail of their lives. But when you're aware of each person as an individual they will appreciate it and respect you for it. Over time, their appreciation will show up in improved performance and operational results.

Regardless of professional rank or status, employees want to know that their leader:

1. Sees them as a person of value.
2. Is interested in seeing them succeed.
3. Cares about their life outside work.

Think carefully about how you view each of the individuals you're responsible for leading. Do they know you see them as a person of value, are interested in their success, and care about their personal life? If you are less than sure of how your employees feel you view them in these three areas, it might be a good time to make some adjustments to your personal style. It is never too late to make positive changes when it involves people.

Prioritizing people takes a personal commitment on the part of every leader. Succeed in this area and not only will most regular folks consistently give you a good effort, but when you're gone they might even remember your name.

Which brings us to a leadership practice that is no less important and works hand-in-hand with what we just discussed.

EVERYONE HAS A NAME. USE IT

Here is something that is guaranteed to make a positive difference in your relationship with people. Whenever possible, refer to them by name. People take notice of those who know their name, and they can't help but respond positively. When you call someone by name, it's a sign that you view him or her as a person of value.

Think about the opposite. If someone feels you are connected either personally or professionally, but you rarely refer to the person by name, it indicates that you may not place much importance on that individual. If the person is one of your employees, it sends a message that you may see him or her as just an employee and not someone important enough for you to learn or speak their first name. And if their name happens to be clearly printed on the name tag they are wearing, that is even more of a missed opportunity.

When I was about twelve, I recall Dad telling Mom at the supper table that a man he'd known for ten or fifteen years "has never one time called me by my name!" It was obvious that my dad didn't hold that gentleman in as high regard as he might have otherwise.

Several years ago, all Sam's Clubs (known then as Sam's *Wholesale* Club) received a shipment of new associate name tags along with instructions to begin using them immediately. They were bright blue and fluorescent orange, and about four times larger than the previous name tags. The associates absolutely hated wearing them!

In an effort to avoid a minor uprising, I called the home office and shared with the executive in charge of our entire operation how much the associates hated those darn oversized name tags. I asked if we could please go back to using the previous, smaller version. Ron told me that Sam had personally requested larger name tags because he couldn't see the associates' names on the old ones. Needless to say, the large name tags stayed.

That wasn't the first or only time the man who was known to his associates as Mr. Sam made clear how important it was that he be able to call the associates by name whenever possible. You can imagine how folks loved it when our chairman spoke their name. Hearing him say your name made you feel appreciated, like you were a meaningful part of things. Referring to associates by name also went a long way toward endearing our founder to the regular folks. I doubt that was his plan. Rather, it was a byproduct of simply treating people with respect. In any regard, it had an impact on how the associates viewed him and it set a good example for his leadership team.

The biggest lesson I learned on this subject, however, occurred when I was given operating responsibility over a group of stores that included most of those in Mississippi and Louisiana. On my first visit to our store in Thibodaux, Louisiana, the store manager, George, told me one of his associates wanted to meet me. I walked over to this gentleman, introduced myself, and referred to him as Sid, the name that was printed on his name tag. Sid said, "Mr. Russ, it's an honor to meet you." He then asked if it would be possible to have his picture taken with me.

Understand that I knew full well I was not a big deal. But having started my career in Sid's shoes, I knew that from a store associate's perspective, the position I held was viewed as a big deal. I was also aware that Sid didn't know me from Adam Sandler. For all he knew, I might be the biggest BOONHAG who'd ever flown on a company plane. But he had an obvious respect for the responsibility I held and the job title that went with it. I told him I'd be honored to have my picture taken with him, providing we took two so I could keep one for myself.

Shortly after, an associate showed up with a camera (this was in the pre-smartphone era) and took our picture. I wrote Sid's name on my copy and put it in my pocket. When I returned to my office later in the week, I pinned the picture to the wall beside my desk, where it stayed for the remainder of my career. The photo reminded me that when I was visiting stores, I was representing our company, our culture, and the principles we were founded on. Every time I looked at the picture, I realized once again that the regular folks looked up to those who held leadership positions. Pinning Sid's picture on my wall turned out to be one of the best things I ever did.

If you attended business school and majored in general management or maybe comprehensive leadership, you might have gotten the idea that success as a manager depends on technical, analytical, or even organizational skills. Those are important, of course. But one of the most important, and effective, things you can do as a manager is to conduct yourself in a way that results in getting people behind you, which starts by learning their first name. *Never underestimate the impact you have on people when they hear you speak their name. It matters!*

A few months later, on my next visit to the Thibodaux store, I was talking on the phone in the receiving office. I sensed someone standing behind me. When I got off the phone, I turned around and found myself standing eye-to-eye with Sid, the man whose picture hung on my office wall. Before I could speak, he said, "Hello, Mr. Russ. Do you remember me?" I responded, "Sid Tabor, of course I remember you!"

I won't soon forget the expression on Sid's face as he looked down at his name tag, which he had covered with his right hand. He stared at his hand for a moment, apparently confirming that his name was fully blocked. Then he looked back at me with tear-filled eyes. He said, "I can't believe you remember me!"

He mentioned that he had something to show me and walked me to his locker. "I'm just an old man," he said, "just an associate, and I've never had an important job or done anything real important." He went on to say, "When I'm gone, I want to leave my kids and grandkids something to remember me by, something that will make them proud."

He opened his locker and took out a photo album that was about five inches thick. He opened the album and in the middle of the first page was the picture that had been taken of the two of us. When I saw what he'd written below the picture, I was blown away: "The day I met Walmart Regional Vice-President Russ Robertson." I was speechless.

Sid continued turning the pages of his life's scrapbook, revealing assorted items and trinkets, many of which related to the few years he'd spent as a Walmart associate. It was a humbling and impactful experience. The memory of this associate's response to an "important" company executive remembering and speaking his name is indelibly imprinted on my memory.

One of the simplest, easiest things any of us can do is to greet someone using their first name. It is especially easy to do when they're wearing it. "Hello, Morris. It's good to meet you. My name is Olivia." Oftentimes all it takes to make a positive impact on your employees is for you to make a small effort, such as referring to them by their name.

I'll never forget Sid or his reaction to what was, in my mind, a small gesture. But as I looked through his scrapbook, I realized it was far more than that to Sid. Thank you, Sid Tabor, for reminding us all of what really matters to regular folks—which includes most of us.

7

What's in It
for Everyone?

Earlier we discussed the fact that most regular folks are not initially motivated by the same things that drive executives. Regular folks don't worry nearly as much as you do about supply-chain management, balance sheets, and return on shareholders' equity.

Most employees show up at work to earn a living to support their families. In the best of circumstances they also are motivated to do a good job.

Every manager wants associates who focus on the customer and the top and bottom lines. However, most employees won't develop these values unless managers show them that what they do in their job impacts the company's financial performance. It also helps when you give them a piece of the pie.

Leaders do themselves a big favor when they make it clear to everyone they lead that as the organization prospers, so will the

employees. What is good for the corporate profit-and-loss statement also will be good for employees at every level of the organization. Leaders make it harder to meet goals when they don't keep
this message in front of their associates.

Although studies have shown that money is not the primary
thing that motivates the average human being, I've found that the
lack of money can be a huge motivator for someone who wants to
earn more of it. When you explain what employees can do to put
more money in their wallets, most will give a good effort toward
your overall plan. That is, as long as the expectations are reasonable
and are communicated by someone they respect. (Recall what we
discussed in the previous chapter about valuing people and even
speaking to them by name.)

You should also know that few regular folks go to work each
day with the objective of doing all they can to help their employer
make a bunch of money. And I've never heard of anyone who was
motivated in a positive direction after reading in their company's
annual report that each of the top five most highly compensated
executives in the company made more money the previous year
than most of the company's employees will make over the course of
a lifetime.

To have a realistic chance at relating to most of the regular folks
on your payroll, consider this: There are a lot more people barely
getting by than there are high wage earners. Far and away, the majority of people who work for a living routinely spend one hundred
percent of the last paycheck before they receive the next one.

With that as background, it's critical that your employees understand why it's in their personal interest to consistently give good effort. Associates and employees who understand they're working for more than just a paycheck are also more likely to have a positive influence on your customers' experience.

Also consider this: Depending on the industry you're in, many of your employees could likely replace their job with one that pays similar wages someplace else. If wages are about the same between your place and the other place, and your employees aren't aware of the overall advantages associated with working for your place, they'll be more likely to jump ship as soon as someone from the other place comes along and offers them a little more money. But motivated associates who have a good understanding of what's in it for them spend less time wondering about what it might be like to work some place else than employees who do not have that understanding.

How Results Impact Employees

If you own or manage a convenience store, you would probably like to know that every employee in your operation comes to work every day with the intention of providing world-class customer service to everyone who enters the store. That is also the goal of virtually every CEO of every organization in the world, regardless of the industry they are in. Getting anywhere close to achieving that goal would clearly set most organizations apart from all the rest. But if the people on your payroll don't understand how providing superior customer service impacts the financials for the place they work, and ultimately their own pay and benefits, most will deliver only a basic level of service. Leaders who understand this are much more likely to have satisfied customers who are willing to wait in line to give them money.

For a long period of time my former company set itself apart from most of its industry peers by instituting a financial-incentive program known as The Profit Sharing Plan. In the seventies and eighties and well into the nineties, it was common to hear associates remark how some occurrence in their store or work area would benefit or hurt their profit-sharing account.

It was a simple, straightforward way for all associates to participate in the financial success of the organization, once they met the criteria for participation. That criteria was not difficult to meet. Once the employee became eligible, participation was automatic. If they chose not to participate (I personally never ran across anyone who chose not to) they had to request that in writing. This is further proof that most regular folks will not turn down money if you offer it to them.

Contributions were made at the end of each fiscal year based on the percentage of net profit achieved in the corporation. Every associate in the plan received a distribution of money to their account based on a percentage of their annual gross income. The percentage was the same for everyone, regardless of the position they filled in the company. It was an effective plan and created a great deal of enthusiasm over a long period of time.

It worked because a boatload of store managers and district managers taught their associates (employees) how each of their roles impacted the company's bottom line. Since the majority of the assets in the profit-sharing plan were invested in our company's stock, most associates gave a good effort once they understood how things tied together financially to ultimately impact the value of their stock in the company. All it really took was teaching the regular folks how things tied together financially. And it doesn't take a PhD to understand that concept.

There's no doubt in my mind that the profit-sharing plan had a significant impact on our effectiveness at generating an atmosphere of ownership throughout the organization. It made a difference toward long-term employee retention, and as a result of the plan's consistent growth over a lot of years also contributed to a number of early retirements.

Leaders who achieve top results oftentimes know how important it is that everyone understand how company performance comes back to benefit them as an individual. These leaders place a priority on doing things to perpetuate an atmosphere of understanding regarding pay and benefits, as well as all other available incentive programs. Employees do not have to know how to read a balance sheet or understand the fine points of mergers and acquisitions. You merely have to teach them the basics of how money flows through your operation and how a portion of that money ultimately shows up in an account or on a check with their name on it.

As an example, teach your employees how selling more of an item with a high gross margin (the profit on an item before expenses are factored in) puts more money "in the bank." Then share with them the various ways the additional money might get put to use. When you explain that the actions and decisions of employees can add profit to your business, and they understand how that impacts their overall compensation and opportunities for advancement, they'll be more likely to do all they can to help improve results.

And if your employees don't have at least a basic understanding of what drives your company financially as well as how those results impact their pay and benefits, how can you possibly expect to compete with an organization that is chock full of people who do understand this concept?

The majority of leaders I ran across who made this concept part of their personal style more times than not were individual unit managers (store and warehouse-club managers). Oftentimes the managers who were the best at it were the highly experienced ones. They had learned that it doesn't do much good to put a pie in front of people if you don't first explain how they can go about getting a piece of it.

The man credited with generating one of the greatest business success stories of the past 75 years had a clear understanding of this leadership concept. He knew that when people understand what's in it for them, all you really have to do is provide them a leader with the skills we're discussing in this book and point them in the right direction. More times than not, they will enthusiastically go get it done!

If you want to find out how well the average employee in your area of responsibility understands how their role affects the financials for your mutual company, ask a few of them. If they look at you like you just fell off a wagon, that's your first clue that they may not understand very much about it. And please keep in mind that when they don't have at least a general understanding of how their role affects financial results and ultimately their pay, benefits, and opportunity for advancement, it's not their fault, it's *your* fault.

Commit this to memory: *People perform at their best when they clearly understand everything that's in it for them.*

WHAT'S THE PLAN AND HOW DOES EVERYONE FIT IN?

The odds of achieving success in an organization increase significantly when everyone knows and understands the current plan for moving forward. This may seem too obvious to mention. But often it's the seemingly obvious things we tend to overlook. You may feel your employees understand the big-picture plan. But do they also understand what the plan is right now, this evening, and for perhaps the next few days?

I'll say this again: When you lead people, you should *never* assume anything important. And that goes double when we're talking about any aspect of your plan. You probably know where you want your company or business unit to be in the next quarter, the next fiscal year, and maybe even the next five years or more. But don't assume that your employees will somehow absorb that information by osmosis, especially if your company or your part of the business is spread out over a large area.

Here's a straightforward way to execute a plan, whether the plan is for the day or the next several years:

1. Determine what the plan is.
2. Commit your soul[1] to executing the plan at the highest possible level.
3. Take the necessary steps to ensure the plan is clearly articulated to every person in your organization who has the potential to contribute to its success.
4. Ensure that everyone in every role at every level has a crystal-clear understanding of what is expected of them.
5. Stay relentlessly focused on the most critical aspects of the plan, and always respond appropriately when your folks execute it, as well as when they don't.

WHAT EFFECTIVE LEADERS DO WELL

I am confident that people who have led companies from start-up to greatness have had, among other qualities, a good business plan. And even more critical to their eventual success, they possessed the ability to keep the vast majority of leaders in their organization focused perpetually on that plan.

You maximize the chances of executing your plan at a high level when everyone in your organization knows what the plan is and what their role is in achieving it.

Like the rest of us, I imagine Sam Walton had shortcomings. I have yet to meet anyone who doesn't. But he was an absolute *master* at keeping people throughout his organization focused on buying merchandise at the lowest possible cost and selling it at a price that was, on average, lower than that of the competition while still achieving a reasonable gross profit. He also was a master at keeping the people who operated his stores focused on driving merchandise sales in a customer-friendly atmosphere and with the lowest feasible operating cost, while understanding what was in it for them when they did.

As the numbers indicate, he may have been at least as good as anyone who's ever drawn breath at getting people behind a business plan. As a testament to the impact of his relentless focus on, and passion for, the business plan he put together in 1962, that same plan in great measure lives on today, more than two decades after his passing.

Regardless of the industry or endeavor, it should be every leader's objective to generate an atmosphere that results in every individual on your team *willingly* doing all they can to help execute the plan. It starts with every person's knowing and understanding the plan as well as their role in it. If you, as a leader, settle for anything less, good luck in achieving the financial results called for in your business plan.

---

[1] Note: The word *soul* is used metaphorically to emphasize the point. If you are in the ministry, however, you might want to take it literally.

8

Don't Expect Employees
to Read Your Mind

The concept of communicating clearly with employees is simple enough, but not many of us are good at it. You could spend years studying this subject. You can even get a PhD in communications if you have the time, money, and inclination. If you're running a business, however, you could just try the time-proven approach of speaking and writing clearly and, when appropriate, in the fewest words possible. Clarity and brevity go far in getting your point across. And make it your goal to get your point across in a respectful manner that leaves no room for misinterpretation, especially when the information is important and/or will touch on a difficult topic.

I recall two leaders who tried, at different times, to communicate the same message to my team. Rather than being clear and getting right to the point, they chose to take the longer way around. Having to guess what they were trying to say, and attempting to interpret their expectations, was frustrating and non-productive for everyone.

The first time this happened, I was managing a Walmart store. We had a new regional vice-president, and toward the end of a store tour he stopped at the end of the greeting-card aisle. He mentioned that setting up a display of Scotch tape in front of giftwrap would generate impulse sales. I said, "That's a good idea." I was agreeing with him. He then shouted, *"I don't see it!"* He was staring at me as if I'd said something derogatory about his mother. Considering my ability to read between the lines had yet to fully develop, I had no idea why he reacted that way, although it was obvious he wasn't happy about something.

A number of months later I had a similar experience with another individual. I was managing Sam's Club #8244 in Houston when we received a visit from our new chief of operations. The man had a longstanding reputation for being difficult to please. His first tour of our operation went all right for the most part, but when he left it was obvious that he was less than completely satisfied. He came back about a week later, and it was a repeat of the earlier visit. I followed him through our building while making note of everything he said. For the second time, he became agitated. All I could think was *What the snot is he always getting so darned worked up about?*

He then pointed out something I thought was petty. In frustration, I called out to one of my assistant mangers. "Jim, get a pallet jack and straighten those pallets out. *Right now!*"

The new chief turned around, pointed his finger at my chest, looked me in the eye, and said, *"That's* what I'm looking for!"

I was no rocket mechanic, but I finally got it. He and the regional vice-president from the previous incident wanted store managers to respond to their input immediately rather than waiting until they left our store. This was not unreasonable. Once we understood it, most of us made the adjustment pretty quickly. In fact, it almost became a game to see how quickly we could get things accomplished during a visit from a supervisor.

The next time this executive conducted a tour of our operation, I instructed five or six associates to follow a few feet behind us. As soon as the executive would point out something, I or a member of my management team would instruct one of the associates to execute the task immediately. It was simply a matter of us understanding the expectation.

BEST RESULTS OCCUR FROM CLEAR COMMUNICATION

Few things are more frustrating in business than not knowing what someone expects from you. It can be your boss, a peer, or someone who reports to you. I was once put in charge of an area of our company at a time when I knew very little about that business unit. I had always wondered what these folks did; now I was in charge of a group of them.

On my first day in the new role, I sat down with the person I would report to and asked what my area was responsible for. I also asked about their expectations of the team and me personally. My new boss responded, "I want you to figure that out." I felt my question must have been misunderstood, so I asked it a little differently the second time. Again the response was "I want you to figure that out."

I left that office dumbfounded. My new leader thought I was either a lot smarter than I was or not quite bright enough to mess things up. Either way, I still didn't know what the heck I was actually responsible for, what my new team really did, or what was expected of me.

In contrast, I once reported to a person who, on the first day we worked together, gave me a reasonably comprehensive overview of my responsibilities. He then told me that, when he asked for something to be done, he expected me to jump on it immediately. He added that whenever I noticed anything that needed to be done, he expected me to jump on it even faster. He was so clear and concise with communicating his expectations that even I was able to understand what he was looking for.

Clarity and brevity. Be specific, to the point, and unambiguous. The best way to inspire performance that meets your expectations is to express your expectations clearly and with respect for the other person. No matter how honorable your intentions, when you leave room for misinterpretation regarding responsibilities, expectations, and objectives, you're missing your best opportunity to execute your program at a high level. You also are missing a chance to help others develop to their full potential.

People crave clear and concise communication from the people to whom they're accountable. Becoming an effective communicator will set you apart from the majority. And the regular folks will appreciate you for not putting them in the position of having to try to read your mind.

If, for example, you want someone to paint a wall red, ask that person to paint the wall red. If you determine that the exact shade is not critical to the project, leave that decision to the person charged with getting it done. If the length of time also is important, give the person with the paintbrush a clear idea of about how long you think it should take. Even better, ask the employee how long he or she thinks it should take to complete the project. In doing that, along with giving them some autonomy regarding the exact color, you will have a much better chance of getting the person's enthusiastic buy-in and sense of ownership.

And if you want the very best shot at getting the wall painted by the deadline, and in the best possible shade of red, explain why the red wall is important to your mutual business. When they understand what's in it for them, they'll more times than not paint the wall a wonderful, eye-catching red and do a great job of it. And pretty darn quickly.

If you choose the path of indirection in communicating with your employees, count on there being confusion and slow followthrough. Your associates are not mind readers, and you should never expect them to be. If you want to improve as a leader who makes clear what the expectations are, make a concentrated effort to speak and write clearly, in a respectful but straightforward manner. Leave out the fluff, don't forget to dot the i, and when possible, try to keep it to the equivalent of one page. Even entry-level employees appreciate getting a summary of priorities and expectations versus an executive thesis.

When leaders fail to clearly convey their thoughts and expectations, the result oftentimes is frustration, missed opportunities, and potential loss of business. Commit yourself to making every effort to be known as a leader who leaves no room for misinterpretation.

9

TMS (Too Much Stuff)

Priorities are conveyed with the most weight and received with the highest level of urgency when they are limited in number. Issuing too many priorities seems to occur when goals are not being met and results are falling short of expectations. When things are going less than outstanding, leaders often respond with too many new initiatives designed to address shortcomings. I call this tendency TMS (Too Much Stuff). Too Much Stuff comes close to being an ironclad guarantee that you will not achieve the result you are going for.

The downside to TMS is that it dilutes the message and blurs the lines between what's important and what's critical. If everything is a priority, soon nothing is a priority.

Another problem with this approach is that over time, employees lose sight of the big picture. They are overwhelmed by directives and emphases to the point that the main thing is no longer the main thing. In fact, the main thing is not even still in view. It got buried under a pile of too many other main things.

Giving out an overabundance of direction to your people—whether for the day or longer range—will have the effect of teaching your employees to not think for themselves. When this occurs, everyone with a vested interest in your endeavor loses. You're not likely to reach the top of your industry's leader board if your primary expectation of the folks you employ is that they become real good at completing tasks and checking off lists.

You hamstring your employees when you load them down with too long a list of things that must get done. They become so worried about not overlooking a single priority that they aren't concentrating on customer service, seeking more efficient ways of doing their job, and strategies to increase sales and reduce costs. You lose the benefit of your employees' creativity, initiative, and self-generated motivation.

To avoid developing a company full of robotic followers, foster an atmosphere that gives associates the autonomy to use their judgment as to what is most important in a given situation. If the choice is between servicing a customer's needs or checking to see if Priority 37 has been taken care of, you would of course want your folks to serve the customer. But on the few things you deem absolutely critical priorities, you want them to understand that your expectation is nothing less than one-hundred percent execution. Regular folks employed in this type of atmosphere learn to think beyond company directives. They'll also take more ownership in their part of the business, as well as more pride in the results they help produce.

As good as my former company was, and probably still is, we

often over-communicated with our operating units. When we did this, it put many of our store and warehouse-club managers, especially the newer ones, in the position of wondering what was most important. Executives would unintentionally water down the priorities by communicating noncritical "to-dos" at the same time as the important stuff. At times we simply made too many things a priority. The cause of this behavior may have originated from a culture that was deeply rooted in making things happen and getting everything done *right now.* Standing around waiting simply was not an acceptable behavior.

And giving too little direction can be just as counterproductive as giving out too much. Somewhere closer to the middle is usually what ends up working best.

When you become effective at communicating the right stuff in the right quantity with the appropriate emphasis, execution on top priorities will improve. You'll also be developing trust and ownership throughout your operation.

THE POWER OF HONESTY AND ACCOUNTABILITY

Along with keeping things clear regarding priorities, there is the proven power of communicating honestly with the people in your life. At the same time, we all recognize that saying things straight, to the point, and truthfully is sometimes difficult, especially when the subject matter is potentially negative.

There's an old saying: "There is no comeback for the truth."

I've found this to be true. I decided years ago that I would always try my best to tell the truth. I have found that regular folks typically respond very well to the truth, providing it's delivered tactfully and from someone they respect. Most problems that result from speaking the truth seem to arise when the person delivering the message uses poor judgment regarding "tact, tone, and timing."

I learned a lasting lesson after I realized I was not as effective at leading people as I'd thought. Although the leadership team I was a part of had been giving our all, our operation was struggling. We were failing to meet basic operational standards. As the person in charge, I understood it was on me and no one else.

After struggling to come up with workable solutions, I felt physically and emotionally spent. For at least the second time in my career, I was giving serious thought to throwing in the towel. After coming home late one night from my job, I shared with my wife my plans to quit this line of work. Sue said, "I know what your problem is: You're not holding your management team accountable." I told her if there was one thing I *was* doing, it was holding them accountable. She then asked, "Are they accomplishing what you're expecting of them?"

It took a minute for that to sink in. When it did, I had a dramatic moment of clarity.

Over time, the lessons I learned led to these principles of accountability: *Be honest with people and clearly communicate your expectations. Upfront, tell folks what you expect of them and clearly explain the details. Communicate tactfully, but with crystal clarity, what you stand for and what you will not stand for. Be straight-*

forward, but never come across as threatening or you will lose their respect. And never lower the bar so one person can get over it unless you're willing to lower the bar for everyone.

After my epiphany, but before I stepped foot back in my operation, I sat down *individually* with each person who reported directly to me. I started each conversation by apologizing for certain aspects of my leadership, specifically for my having been less than clear about what was expected and for being demanding without holding each of them accountable for the expected results. I committed to changing that part of my behavior immediately.

I then asked each of my direct reports to share with me their career goals and what they expected of our company and of me personally.

Then I drew the clearest picture I could regarding the expectations going forward. We discussed what they could and should expect from me and, of course, what I expected of them. I didn't put my expectations off on anyone else, nor did I use some higher up as leverage. I made it entirely about each of them in light of my unbending expectations, and our working together as a leadership team to execute fully in each of our roles.

I spoke in a respectful, but straightforward, manner. I left no major stone unturned and absolutely no room for misinterpretation. We discussed the potential consequences that might result from their future leadership, the acceptable time frames for improving results, and my personal intentions as their direct leader.

These were not easy conversations, but they were wonderfully productive. One member of our team who had spent several years as an officer in the military, as well as a few years in private-sector business, told me that "not one time" had anyone ever explained to him so clearly and specifically what he was responsible for. He also shared that it was the first time anyone had asked what he personally expected of his immediate superior. (*Superior* was his word choice, not mine.) He was enthusiastic, not upset. I knew then that, regarding leading and communicating in the workplace, I had discovered something that really did matter to regular folks like me.

I'll always remember the feeling I had: I felt reborn as a leader!

I learned that, given the opportunity, most people want to be a part of something special and will rise to the occasion when they clearly understand what you expect. Regular folks respond well to high expectations, providing they know the expectations. And I discovered that people appreciate being held accountable for high standards of performance and overall behavior, providing everyone is held to that same level of accountability.

As a result of this painful, but life-changing, experience, I made a few key adjustments to my leadership style. If you're somewhat new to the concept of complete honesty and true accountability, you may consider trying this:

1. Write down your expectations of the people who report to you, being as detailed as you want. (You are paid to lead, so you have a right to establish the expectations.)

2. *Sit down one-on-one with each of your direct reports, when each of you can focus one-hundred percent on the conversation.*

3. Ask each one to share his or her goals, as well as what they expect of you as the leader.

4. Share the details of your expectations (see 1. above).

5. Going forward, be relentless about following through with your direct reports, giving them consistent personal input and feedback regarding how they are performing. Do this individually with each one and do it often.

6. Take appropriate action regarding their overall performance, recognizing when expectations are met and of course when they're not.

7. Adjust as necessary.

The power of honesty while holding people accountable for achieving results is nearly unbelievable. When you are tactfully honest with those you lead, and when they have a clear understanding of your expectations, it results in an atmosphere where underperformance has nowhere to hide.

10

Make Work Enjoyable
for Everyone

The man who invented my old company oftentimes reminded us that the best compliment you can be paid, if you are a part of the organization he started, is when someone says, "You're a great merchant."

I have no way of knowing today whether he meant that literally. But of the numerous times I heard him say this in person, he spoke those words with passion. My perception was that, to our founder, being great merchants was one of the major keys to success in the business we were in. Repeating this over and over may have been just one more way he had of emphasizing the importance of staying focused on anything and everything that had to do with buying and selling merchandise.

Like all good leaders, he backed up what he said by always staying focused on the merchandise we sold or could be selling. As an example, any time he attended a meeting of just about any type or size, you could bet he was going to talk about a great item he saw in a competing store. Or he would mention one of our stores that had sold an amazing quantity of something. Or he might recognize someone for an outstanding achievement having to do with something they had bought or sold.

But each time I heard him or any of our executives say that being a great merchant was the highest compliment anyone could pay you at our company, I always felt differently about it. From my view, the greatest compliment anyone could pay another person in nearly any endeavor that involves people is to say, "You're a great leader, with the ability to inspire folks in the right direction."

Sam was both a great merchant and an outstanding inspirational leader, but few individuals possess that combination of talents. You can be the greatest merchant the world has ever seen, but if you can't generate an atmosphere that inspires others to do their best work at selling, your impact will be limited primarily to the things you're good at and that you can personally touch. In contrast, great leaders multiply and expand their effectiveness by motivating and inspiring regular folks to achieve goals and generate results.

With that in mind, we need to look more carefully at how to develop a work environment that feels less like work and more like a good way to spend a day while getting paid for it.

Over the years, I've worked with and around a good number of stiff shirts who tended to take nearly everything too seriously. They either didn't know how or weren't willing to loosen up, even when it was called for. Some were the kind of folks who might have a difficult time distinguishing between what's funny and what's romantic in a romantic comedy. A few seemed as if they were on an unending quest to make the work environment as stale and uninspiring as possible.

I'm not suggesting that work should be a circus or that leaders should spend their time entertaining the employees. But if you are the person in charge, step back from time to time, take a breath, and try to recall what it was like to be an employee working in a regular job and just getting by. What were some of the reasons you enjoyed coming to work back when you were more like a regular person?

There's no doubt that for some leaders, establishing an enjoyable, yet productive, work environment does not come naturally. But with a committed effort, even a person who rarely gets the punch line can accomplish this if they make doing so a priority. Enjoyment and productivity are two atmospheric qualities that do not have to be mutually exclusive.

But don't take my word for it. Look at the work environment you're in right now. Does it feel like a job or more often like an enjoyable way to spend a day? How about your last job and the one before that?

Now think about the person who has the greatest influence over your workday. Does she or he inspire you to give your best effort, and do you enjoy being around that person? If you're hesitating on this answer, do you cringe when your immediate supervisor walks into the room? How about the people who report to you?

Are they inspired under your leadership, or do they grow silent and on guard every time you come around?

Some might feel that trying to make work fun is either a waste of time or evidence that you are not focused on the right things. But I know for a fact it's possible for leaders to conduct themselves in a way that sets the tone for a healthy, enjoyable, and *productive* business atmosphere. I have worked in settings where most of the people involved were inspired to give their best effort. The atmosphere we worked in motivated us, and it was due almost entirely to the immediate leadership.

In each of those instances, the people in charge were effective at communicating the company objectives. Those leaders held everyone to high standards of performance, execution, and behavior. Most went out of their way to recognize the folks who were doing the work. They treated everyone with respect and showed that they saw each employee as an individual rather than just another person in a crowd.

The leaders also did things that made it fun to be at work. Sometimes those things had little, if any, direct connection to the business we were in. But regular folks appreciate knowing their leaders are like them in terms of enjoying life. And when a leader will, from time to time, demonstrate that not every situation involved with the business is a life-or-death issue, employees feel good about working there.

We had quite a few people, even executives, who demonstrated the kind of leadership ability I just described. One was a guy who for years ran our store-planning division. He was an exceptional communicator and one of the most decisive and inspirational leaders I've ever been around. He was serious about his leadership responsibilities and the role his people played in the company. But when it came to establishing a productive yet enjoyable work atmosphere, he was as good at it as anyone.

As an example, he once dressed up in a ridiculous cowboy outfit in front of a large group of associates and performed a silly skit that tied in to the company's focus at the time. It made everyone laugh and showed that he was human.

He was the same leader who once, on the spur of the moment, crawled inside a dunk tank at a fundraising event held outside the home office. He was wearing a nice suit, dress shoes, and assorted accoutrements which indicated that he had not planned on participating in this way. But when he found out the event had gotten off to a slow start, he didn't hesitate before getting inside that tank, fully clothed, to help raise the level of participation. It wasn't long before he was under water, and all the regular folks present got a big kick out of it.

Afterward, it was apparent he had likely ruined his suit and shoes. But as a person who understood the impact that each leader has on the work atmosphere, he gladly made a personal sacrifice for the greater good of that particular event, as well as for the enjoyment of all the regular folks who attended it.

You can probably imagine how the associates under his guidance loved and respected him. Having earned a reputation as a leader who cared about the people he led and the company they all worked for, all he had to do was explain the plan, point his folks in the direction he wanted them to go, and turn them loose. They would gladly get it done. And if there happened to be a brick wall in the way, his folks would run through it, not around it. If you've ever heard the slogan "Our people make the difference," it referred to leaders such as him, as well as the regular folks he was leading!

LEADERS ARE RESPONSIBLE
FOR THE ATMOSPHERE, GOOD OR BAD

I also have been in work environments that were anything but enjoyable, and it always came down to the leadership. The tone was set by the way the person in charge behaved, communicated, and treated folks.

I worked around a few people who were so out of touch, they said things like "Do you know I can fire you?" "If you can't get it done, I'll find someone who can!" and "As long as you do what I tell you, we'll get along just fine." These are the kinds of things that leaders rarely need to vocalize. When you say or write things such as this, the result will be the opposite atmosphere of the one you may be trying to achieve.

Even less effective than a leader who demotivates the employees is a leader people feel they can't trust. I experienced that only one time and it was a terrible feeling. Working around someone you deem untrustworthy takes nearly all the enjoyment out of work and results in a very uncomfortable atmosphere. An employee's lack of trust in a leader not only takes most of the fun out of things, it ultimately results in a lack of productivity. If employees sense that a leader is someone who can't be trusted, they'll spend a great deal of time trying to protect themselves from that person. They'll be so guarded they won't be able to think clearly about putting their best energies toward the critical functions of their job. Their best energies will go toward self-preservation, which accomplishes nothing positive for any work group or organization.

If you're in charge, it's primarily up to you to establish the atmosphere in your area of responsibility. *If you are the leader and your employees do not enjoy being at work, it's mostly because of you. Likewise, you deserve some credit if the majority of the people in your employ feel good about being there. The responsibility for establishing that atmosphere is on your shoulders. You don't have to do it all yourself, but it begins and ends with the person in charge.*

If you're running an operation and have the self-awareness to know you can't relate to your average employee, then determine which of your key managers has that skill. Ask them to step up in those areas. Explain your objective and the importance of the leadership role you want them to play. You'll be doing everyone a favor when you ask people to accentuate the areas where they excel, especially when what they are good at complements areas where you have gaps.

When you're effective at generating a satisfying work atmosphere, your associates will do better work and they'll be more likely to stay with you when times are tough. Unhappy people are much more likely to jump ship during the rough times all businesses go through from time to time.

It has also been my experience that most folks have an appreciation for people who can occasionally poke some fun at themselves or allow someone else to do it for them. I've found this to be true especially when those people are in a position of leadership. Let me share an example.

I received my twenty-year service award with my former company during a Saturday-morning meeting, the one made famous by our founder and attended by large crowds of associates from around the company every Saturday morning at 7:30. My leader brought me up in front of the crowd and, after making some comments, presented me with a certificate of appreciation along with the microphone he had previously held.

Of course, most of us were aware that the three executive signatures on these certificates were produced by a printer. With that in mind, I had decided ahead of time that I was going to get mine signed personally and, in the process, have a little fun at the expense of our top two leaders.

After making a few sincere remarks, I looked over at our CEO and our Vice-Chairman, referred to them by their first names, and said, "Oh yeah, one more thing. I couldn't help but notice that these signatures appear to have been produced on a printer." The crowd started humming with snickers and muffled laughter.

I went on to say, "If it's not too much trouble (I paused for effect), would you guys mind actually signing this thing?"

That comment brought the house down and to the credit of our top executives they were laughing just as much as anyone!

They continued indulging the crowd by reading aloud my

prepared statements which, of course, extolled me as the individual most responsible for their individual business successes.

The result of their good nature was a spontaneous, rousing, standing ovation for them and, I believe, for a shared moment of the not-so-serious side of our company culture. Interestingly, this type of silly occurrence was not out of the ordinary in my former company.

If you are a professional leader, you probably take your responsibility seriously. You should. But don't fail to realize that the environment your employees work in has a direct effect on their productivity. Foster the right atmosphere, and the regular folks will show their appreciation by giving a strong effort in the role they're in. Your customers will notice the difference and it will soon show up on your bottom line.

11

Don't Give Up on Folks

D o you quickly give up on people when they falter, or will you go to the wall for those who have previously proven their worth and are still making an effort?

The culmination of more than twenty-five years of leading and being led resulted in my spending the final three-and-one-half years of my career responsible for helping store and warehouse-club managers who were going through a difficult time. If you hang around long enough and are responsible for other people in your organization, you will almost certainly face such a time of difficulty.

You can't pin down the cause of leadership ineffectiveness to just one thing. Everything about the person in charge impacts the enterprise for which she or he is responsible. It is during your toughest times as a leader when you have the opportunity to learn the most to become a stronger leader in the future. Learning at this point begins with facing the possibility that regardless of how experienced you might be, you may not have it all figured out. In other words, it takes humility, self-awareness, and a willingness to listen and learn. Admitting to yourself, and even to others, that you have room to improve is a good place to begin.

One of our executive leaders was a person who understood the critical role each unit manager played in the success of our company. He knew that executing our program at a high level depended, more than anything else, on the ability and performance of the individuals who managed our stores, warehouse clubs, and distribution centers. Each had to do a number of things well. But most importantly, they had to create the right atmosphere in their operation while leading in a way that accomplished objectives through others. That sounds so basic it shouldn't need to be stated. But don't brush past it like it doesn't apply to you. It applies to *every* leader at every level.

The key leader I referred to had for many years witnessed the negative impact on our operating units when their manager struggled. Not only that, he knew it could be devastating for the associates when their manager failed and had to be replaced. As a result, he was committed to make every viable effort to minimize leadership failure.

He said he wanted to improve and broaden the scope of an existing training effort, and at the same time change the negative perception that had become associated with it. Rather than our managers having to bear the stigma of failure associated with being chosen for this specific leadership training, he wanted the people who attended to come away feeling good about what they had just gone through.

The new training would be laser-focused on leadership behavior and execution. We wanted the attendees to leave with the realization that their leadership effectiveness depended primarily on their relationship with the people they led as well as their ability to execute the company program within a healthy atmosphere.

The school that was being replaced had been tagged the *Struggling Store Manager School.* You might imagine what it felt like to find out you'd been selected to attend that school.

This senior executive told me that, with the new training effort, we were "by God not going to give up on people!" He told me that he knew I was a leader who placed a high level of importance on people. (This was perhaps the greatest business-related compliment I've ever received.) He went on to say that when you're in a leadership role, being an expert on people has more value to an organization than being an expert on just about anything else. To this day I believe he was right. If you're in a position of leadership, knowing and understanding people is critical to your ability to execute your company's program.

DEVELOP LEADERS WHO WILL FOCUS ON ACCOMPLISHMENT THROUGH OTHERS

As I reviewed the subject matter and agenda from the existing school, it was apparent that the focus was somewhat misplaced.

The content of the previous school was almost exclusively on operational and merchandising concerns. When you're in the business of operating retail stores for the purpose of selling merchandise to make a profit, operational and merchandising issues are of course critical to your business. But I had learned (in spades) over a long period that the primary reason people struggle in leadership roles has more to do with how they interact with people than any other single aspect of their performance. A leader who can keep those they lead motivated and feeling good about the role they fill can overcome most challenges.

When you were made a manager at your current level, it likely had quite a bit to do with your overall knowledge of the business endeavor. But your effectiveness at executing a business plan has more to do with your ability to accomplish things through those you lead—the regular folks—than it does your detailed knowledge of sprockets and widgets or your level of formal education. I believed this then, and I believe it even more strongly today.

Because of this belief, the teaching effort I was put in charge of would be focused on leadership and ultimately on how to execute objectives and achieve goals while respectfully leading the people who do most of the actual work.

We were straightforward with each attendee regarding why they were chosen to attend this training. We changed the name of the school to Career Development Seminar (CDS), which was a small thing. Changing the content was significant.

We were determined to remove the "program" identity because people tend to execute required functions with the same degree of enthusiasm they might bring to bear on filling out a daily asset-protection checklist. We wanted every part of the training to be of critical importance as it touched on the skills of leading people and executing a plan, and we stayed true to our goal.

We spent time only on the things that mattered most to people in everyday, real-world situations. In fact, it covered many of the things you are reading about in this book. This was extraordinarily important in our business because of a leadership truth that we all need to keep in mind: *Everyone struggles at times. Good folks are hard to find and there is not an endless supply of potential replacements. Great leaders don't easily give up on people, especially when there's a decent chance of saving them.*

We held all classes off-campus, completely away from the home office. We didn't want the school to be easily accessible to company folks who might decide to drop in at their convenience. Some of our executives had a tendency to wander around (an effective leadership behavior), and when they found a room with a meeting going on they would oftentimes sit down in the back and listen in. Although "wandering around" and interacting with associates at all levels was a strong aspect of our company culture, for our purposes we didn't want the managers who were attending our school to be intimidated by an "acronym" sitting in the back and listening in on our intimate conversations. And when we invited people to speak with the attendees, we wanted only leaders who had demonstrated selfless characteristics that model good leadership.

As an example of what we *didn't* want, we once heard from a senior officer who spent the entire time talking about himself. He didn't get it: Our school was not about him, it was about the managers. He didn't understand that regular folks aren't impressed by titles alone, and they're even less impressed with how much you might think of yourself and your long list of accomplishments. As a result, he wasn't invited back.

Thankfully, many of our senior leaders fully realized what was important to people. These were leaders who had a positive influence on the folks attending CDS, just as they did whenever they visited with the regular folks throughout our company.

One of our senior operations officers always made it clear when he visited our school that it was *his* honor to be there. He spoke from the heart and talked about things that mattered most to the people who were there. Like many of our best leaders, he had started his career close to the bottom and earned his way up. Prior to joining Walmart in 1986 as an assistant store manager in Pueblo, Colorado, he began his work career at the absolute bottom of a competing company. He also had been a store manager and knew how formidable it was to be charged with total responsibility for a large building sitting on several acres of property, with a multi-million dollar inventory on site. And what it felt like to have direct responsibility for the livelihoods of up to a few hundred individuals and, indirectly, the families who went with them. He also had experienced firsthand the nearly overwhelming responsibility of knowing it's on your shoulders to do everything within reason to maintain your company's hard-earned good reputation in the town in which your store is located.

A store manager has a job description seemingly better suited to a CEO than to an individual unit manager. This leader had not forgotten where he came from and, as a result, he was able to relate well to our class members. As a result of the leader he had proven to be, he had an open invitation to visit our leadership development school any time he could.

GIVING UP IS A BAD EXAMPLE

A few years into our effort we had a management shuffle in the upper echelon of our company and our school fell under the overall influence of a leader who was new to the area. Several weeks after he showed up, I met with him to share what we were doing and how we were doing it, as well as the positive outcomes. I knew that without his support our effort could, at some point, become part of the NFL (Not For Long).

After listening for a few minutes, he said, "Is that it?" I told him that was a brief overview. He then said (with an air of contempt) something very close to "It's fine what you're doing with this school, trying to help managers who aren't doing the job. But let me tell you something: People get *one chance* and they're *out!*" As he said "one chance," he held up his right index finger, ostensibly to drive home his point. Then with the same hand he made a fist, with his thumb pointing up, and thrust it over his right shoulder as he said, *"Out!"* I wasn't the sharpest tool in the shed, but there was no doubt this BOONHAG didn't get it and wasn't going to be supportive of our commitment to not give up on people.

As I walked out of his office, I couldn't help but admit that the new guy didn't understand that we were all on the same team. Neither did he realize that there did not exist an endless supply of people with the overall capabilities and experience to succeed as unit managers in our system. You'll be interested to know that it wasn't too far into the future before the company that we all worked for, fittingly, gave up on *him*.

And the greatest example I've ever witnessed of someone who was committed to not giving up on people was the leader who made the decision to retool our leadership development school in an effort to make it more impactful for those who would attend. Over the time period the school existed, he spoke in person with nearly every group of managers who came through the training. This was not by accident. He made it clear at the beginning that unless he was out of the country, he expected to meet personally with each group of managers who attended. And if that alone doesn't tell the story of his passion for people, then consider that at the time he was one of the top three executives in our entire worldwide organization.

As a leader in any enterprise, when you come across a fellow associate who is going through a difficult time for whatever reason, you have a decision to make. Will you do everything within reason to support their getting back to performing at the acceptable level they were once at? Or will you choose to allow them to fail and just replace them with someone else? Like most other important decisions that leaders face, the choice is yours.

12

Your Expendability Improves Your Operation's Productivity

A worthy goal of every leader would be to eventually become the most expendable person in your operation. There may be short-term job security if employees need your constant input and supervision. But that style of management won't develop many future leaders if everyone is waiting for you to tell them what to do. Teach your employees how and why things need to be done, as well as how outcomes affect them personally. Over time, you will be able to focus more of your efforts on things such as planning and strategizing. You'll also have more time for inspiring, encouraging, and supporting the regular folks while they handle most of the things necessary to achieve overall goals and objectives.

I worked around three individuals in particular, all of whom initially made a positive impression on me as movers and shakers. They were high-energy people and seemed to spend most of their time running around shouting orders and giving direction. It was an effective style as long as they were present to issue orders.

But the thing I learned from watching these leaders was that running around slinging orders and dealing out tasks isn't nearly as effective, over the long term, as teaching people how, explaining why, and discussing the potential outcomes of what they do in the operation.

I know several people who are great at managing in this way. One leader who really stood out was a person who had a long-standing reputation for rolling up his sleeves. Before telling someone to do just about anything important, he would nearly always explain the why's and how's associated with the task. As a result of his ability to teach and develop people, he was invited to move around the company into different areas and capacities. He was so effective at developing others that he eventually worked in business units outside his home country. The people who gave him those opportunities recognized that he was an excellent teacher and developer of people. Instead of expecting folks to memorize instructions or simply follow his directions, he put most of his efforts toward teaching people to understand what they were doing and why.

When I think of the impact this person had on the regular folks he worked with, the thing that comes to mind is something another one of our excellent leaders used to say: "Those who can, teach!"

Those who achieve top results over the long term are those who know how to teach the people they employ. *Focus on teaching and developing associates who understand the business you're in, rather than expecting them to just follow orders or memorize current buzz words and catch-phrases. A leader who can achieve results through others, even when the leader is not physically present, is more valuable than a person who can get things accomplished only when on-site. And leaders who work toward becoming expendable move up...not out.*

This approach toward becoming an expendable leader works at every level. It is not my intent to convince you of Sam Walton's amazing prowess over the course of his life as an exceptional manager and leader. But trust me when I tell you that while he was traveling the country, and even the world, visiting his company's operating units and distribution centers, as well as competitors and other businesses, *no one* was standing around waiting for him to tell them what to do.

When you take time to teach your employees how and why, you'll be developing associates who understand the details of the business. The long-range payoff will be consistent results, even when you're not hovering over the employees. As a side benefit of becoming expendable, you'll have time to think and plan. And if you're not thinking and planning, who is?

DON'T FLAUNT YOUR WEALTH OR STATUS

We had an executive a number of years ago who, on numerous occasions, demonstrated that either he didn't understand or didn't care who our average associates were. That lack of understanding the regular folks prevented a lot of associates from fully respecting this leader over the few years he was there.

On at least two occasions, he went out of his way to share that one of the numerous vehicles he owned was a "very expensive one." If he had avoided this, the regular folks likely would never have known their leader owned a vehicle that cost more than the house many of them lived in.

It may be that his success had gone to his head and, as a result, he lost sight of what really mattered to people regarding those who led them. His actions in those two instances didn't make him a bad person; it was just one more sign that he didn't have a good understanding of what matters to and inspires regular folks.

We had another executive who spent a great deal of time talking about himself, alluding to his ownership of luxury items, the latest high-level person or celebrity he'd been hobnobbing with, and so on. He was otherwise a likable guy and a pretty good leader. But he seemed to have forgotten that it really wasn't about him; it was about the regular folks who did most of the work involved in executing the company plan.

Conversely, we had several leaders who nearly always set a great example in the area of humility. They consistently showed that they understood what really matters to most people. Interestingly, some of these leaders were at the very top of the organization. They rarely talked about themselves, especially in front of regular folks (which is most of us). They *never* talked about what they owned or what they were planning on buying. For the most part, they didn't do "executive profile" interviews for magazines that feature primarily the rich and famous. They didn't share information publicly about their favorite exotic vacation spot, nor did they give media tours of their palatial second homes. As far as I knew, they never made themselves the center of attention. Rather, they always made it about the business we were in and the associates who did the work. Any time the subject was about financial reward (which it rarely was), the discussion was always on what's in it for everyone. It was obvious those leaders still had a good understanding of what it was like to be a regular person.

That kind of behavior tells a story that goes beyond just being humble. It was proof that they understood it wasn't about them or what was in it for them. Rather, it was about all the folks in the organization and what was in it for all of us.

Those are the kinds of traits regular folks are drawn to. People will gladly line up behind you if you consistently make it about them instead of you. Make it about them as much as possible and they'll respond to your leadership. Then, when you're charging the hill, you won't have to look back to see if anyone is behind you.

UNDERSTAND WHY YOU ARE BEING PAID

If you're in a position of leadership for an organization that you don't own and you want to feel liberated from some of the pressures inherent with being in charge, accept the fact that the only reason you're on the payroll is to help execute the company's program.

Unless the condition of your employment is based significantly on your effectiveness at coming up with new ideas or inventing and creating, then it's likely the primary reason you're getting paid is to execute effectively and productively in the role you're in. Your total compensation is likely predicated on your ability to execute the company program within your area of responsibility. And as a leader within an organization, it's important that you don't confuse *your* program with the organization's program. Unless your program fits within the parameters of the company plan, you don't have the right to bring it into the equation.

I recall a memorable example of getting people off their personal program and back on the company program. It occurred when a battle-proven leader named Tom was put in charge of store operations for the flagship division of our organization. Prior to his taking over and for reasons that may be arguable, an atmosphere had developed wherein a handful of significantly empowered operational leaders were essentially running their own program. Any time there was a realignment of store operational responsibilities at the region and division level, the top priorities and key focus items for the stores in many of the regions and divisions would change. The specific changes would depend on who was now over that area.

The new operations chief was one of a handful of people closer to the top than the bottom who understood how frustrating it was for store and district managers when they had to adjust in midstream in order to meet the personal demands and pet priorities of a new leader. He knew that kind of atmosphere wasn't healthy for an organization, especially one set up to operate under a central command structure with one set of overall goals and objectives. And he was a great example of three critical leadership behaviors that were discussed in chapters 4, 5, and 8: Take charge immediately, make clear what you stand for, and don't leave room for misinterpretation, especially on things that are important.

The first thing he did when he reported in his new role was to gather his direct reports and explain that, going forward, there was going to be one program, one set of priorities, and one collaborative effort. Everyone would stay on the same page and would work toward common goals. He made clear that anything short of that was unacceptable.

In relatively short order, he put an end to the days of individual leaders within the same company running their own programs.

After he drew this line in the sand, we were back to one set of objectives. It wasn't long before it showed up, measurably and quantifiably, in the financial results. Getting everyone focused on the company program also had a positive impact on leadership morale. His actions seemed to cut down on the amount of time that operations management, at all levels, spent worrying and speculating as to who their next boss was going to be.

When every individual in your work group or company has a clear understanding of what they are getting paid to do—as well as what they are not getting paid to do—they will be more likely to focus all their energies toward the execution of your company's program.

13

Don't Be
an Arrogant Bully

I've been exposed to a number of people at various leadership levels whose primary style was intimidation. There is no place for this. Simply put, bullying is not a leadership skill and there is no justification for it outside the world of contact sports.

We had a handful of leaders who were well-known for their *techniques of intimidation.* On one occasion, one of these individuals verbally hammered a fellow associate so relentlessly in front of a group that the poor guy passed out cold. I have seen a few leaders at the store, district, region, and division level who seemed to enjoy making folks fear for their jobs. It's beyond me how these individuals ever get put in charge of anything significant, much less are able to stay there for any length of time. But it does happen.

Ultimately, however, it seems the fallout from being a business bully catches up with most who choose it as their primary leadership style. Most regular folks will fear a bully, but they won't have much, if any, respect for one. Personally, I can't think of even one bully I knew who I wanted to be like. On a positive note, their behavior often was an example of how *not* to treat regular folks.

When your employees know you hold the end of the rope that is their family's financial lifeline and you do or say things that cause them to fear you might at any time let go, you are a business bully. Anyone who thinks this is an effective style is out of touch with reality regarding what motivates regular folks.

As a note, I'd be less than forthcoming if I said I've never seen bullying work, at least on a short-term basis. But like other leadership tactics that don't have the best interest of people in mind, intimidation will eventually come back to haunt leaders who use it. And as a word of caution, if you are a business bully and are unwilling to change, you might want to make sure the folks you're leading are in front of you, not trailing along behind you.

BE A STRONG BUT HUMBLE LEADER

If the people you lead perceive you as curt, unapproachable, self-centered, all-knowing, and/or high-and-mighty, you'll have a difficult time gaining their respect and trust. They may give the impression they're on board with your program, and they may even do and say things that cause you to believe they're as excited about you as you are. But that will not hold when you're not looking. Top performers will nearly always give their best effort regardless of who their leader is. But not everyone is a top performer.

And even top performers do better under a strong yet humble leader.

There has been a lot spoken and written about a thing called "servant leadership," and I have met a few people who are actually good at it. I've witnessed examples of leaders with a servant style in numerous roles inside and outside of the company I grew up in. They set a great example in the area of serving those they led. I'm guessing that most companies and associations would like to be able to list servant leadership as one of the benefits of working for or with their organization. Some would be proud if they could honestly say it was a cornerstone of their company culture. I've found that most people are better at talking and writing about it than they are at actually carrying it out. Here's a real-life example of what it looks like in action:

> One morning a few years ago my wife and I walked through the doors of the church we attend. The first two individuals we ran into were the CEO of the largest corporation on the planet and his wife. They were handing out the weekly church bulletin and smiling as they greeted all of us regular folks. They didn't arrive in a limo, they weren't given special seating in the auditorium, and they weren't standing around waiting for someone to serve them. They were serving all of us. It was one of *the greatest* individual examples I have ever personally witnessed of servant leadership.

Humility is the opposite of arrogance or selfishness, and it hardly ever comes naturally. It is human nature to call attention to our accomplishments and to want to occupy the best seats in the house. But if your goal is to be the best leader you possibly can be, remember this: *Be a strong yet humble leader. Leadership arrogance is unbecoming, and regular folks don't want to follow an arrogant leader.*

To this day, the sight of that husband-and-wife team at the entrance of that church building, performing a task typically carried out by substantially less-famous folks, still nearly blows my mind. It also continues to inspire me to be a more humble person and a leader who tries to never forget what matters to most people. And as a side note, the scene I just described was not a one-time occurrence. I've often wondered how frequently anything even remotely like that occurs at the other four hundred ninety-nine Fortune 500 companies scattered throughout the world.

I could share numerous other examples of humility, but I'm confident nearly all of us know humility, as well as arrogance, when we see it. I'm also confident the vast majority of regular folks don't like being around people they perceive as arrogant. They are even less likely to want to be led by an arrogant person.

If arrogance shows up on your personal top-ten list of outstanding qualities, consider working toward removing it from that list. Arrogance simply is not an effective leadership skill. And remember this: Regular folks will *run* from an arrogant boss to line up behind a leader who demonstrates the uncommon qualities of a servant.

GENIUS VS. REGULAR FOLKS

It doesn't hurt to have a few intellectual folks scattered around in the right places. I've run across a handful of individuals in my corporate life who came close to registering on the "scary-smart scale." But the vast majority were more like regular, everyday people. As one of our great, long-time company leaders used to say, "We're just a bunch of ordinary people doing extraordinary things." Although I don't personally recall witnessing a lot of truly extraordinary things, we did seem to routinely do a lot of little things better than many, if not most, of our direct competitors. Perhaps a more accurate description of who we were and what we did would have been "a bunch of mostly regular folks doing *out-of-the-ordinary things.*" Either way, the proof of the extra effort on the part of a bunch of mostly normal people can be found in the numbers, which rarely lie.

Consistently achieving results requires the involvement of a broad mix of people, but not necessarily a boatload of MBAs and PhDs. In my experience, when it came to getting things done and executing a plan, it was usually the regular folks who came up with most of the good ideas and accounted for the lion's share of the output. I doubt anyone at my alma mater has an accurate tally of where most of the good ideas came from between 1962 and today. But over the course of my time there, a large percentage of those ideas were generated by the people who were in the trenches, working hard to carry out the details of the business plan.

Leaders need to be smart enough to listen to the people they lead, regardless of their job title or academic pedigree. A leader who is wise enough to listen to all the folks around her or him can be more valuable to an organization than the combined efforts of several super-smart executives.

Geniuses are necessary if you're building rockets, working with quantum theory, or researching a cure for cancer. However, the work I was involved in was simply selling stuff that was made by other people. We would occasionally complicate things and, as a result, stumble off course now and then. A few times we even fell short of Wall Street expectations. But over a long period, we routinely maintained focus on the things that mattered most.

And what is it that matters most if you are in the business of selling a physical product or service of some kind? People, product, and price. And in that order.

What Now?

The focus in any business is to carry out the company's priorities, to meet goals, and to achieve results that equal or exceed the plan. As we have seen, none of that can be done without the buy-in, commitment, and performance of the people you lead. Knowing how to work with regular folks is key to your success as a leader at any level and in any industry, company, or organization. These are the things we have talked about throughout *Leading Regular Folks*.

When you treat people with respect, help them feel like they're a meaningful part of a worthwhile endeavor, and inspire them in the right direction, most will give you a good effort. Often, it is the regular folks who seem to have a better grasp of what's most important and what works most efficiently and effectively in the workplace. They can be more in touch with what it takes to succeed even than some of the individuals who are charged with ultimate responsibility.

The most effective long-term leaders seem to be those who pay attention to the regular folks and are continually aware of what's on their minds, how they live, and what matters most to them. These leaders treat all people with respect, in all situations and under all circumstances. And they do everything within reason to help their employees and associates feel good about the role they're in.

As you move through your career, you should keep in mind that when you walk out their door for the last time, people are going to remember you not so much for your business accomplishments as for the manner in which you interacted with them and for how you made them feel as an individual in the role they were in.

How leaders behave matters, and it matters all the time!

Author's Note

Thank you for reading my book! The objective was to share meaningful insights that will help you better fulfill your responsibility for leading people. If this objective was achieved, you should now have an adjusted perspective regarding what's actually important to the vast majority of the people around you. The people I call Regular Folks.

If you are interested in learning more about how to achieve your goals by helping those you lead achieve their goals, contact me at LeadingRegularFolks@gmail.com

I would enjoy hearing from you!

Acknowledgments

So many people have had a positive impact on me, my family, and my career that it would take another book just to list your names! Each of you knows who you are, and I hope you know what you have meant to me and my family. But I owe a special debt of gratitude to all the wonderful people I know as associates and partners who worked alongside me and others like me over many years. I acknowledge and appreciate the associates, past and present, of:

WALMART STORES

Stores in far-east Texas as well as in Louisiana, Mississippi, west Alabama, and southeast Arkansas, especially:

194 Rolla, Missouri (before consolidating with #101)
187 Pacific, Missouri (before consolidating with #295)
44 Eldon, Missouri
80 Columbia, Missouri
159 Columbia, Missouri

SAM'S CLUBS

All over the Midwest and South Texas, plus additional stores, especially:

8241 Midwest City, Oklahoma

8244 Houston, Texas (44 The Super Store!)

8251 St. Charles, Missouri

8205 St. Louis, Missouri

8252 Charleston, South Carolina

8182 Manchester, Missouri

Thanks to each of you for working so hard and for teaching me, and others like me, what matters most to regular folks! (And while I'm at it, I'd like to thank another regular person who is not in the business of selling stuff. Ron Lee was the editor of *Leading Regular Folks.* I would like to thank Ron for his excellent support and insight. His fingerprints are all over this book.)

Your former associate and friend,

Russ

About the Author

In 1982 Russ Robertson was the youngest store manager in Walmart. Two years later he was managing the 4th Sam's Club to ever open its doors, where his team of hard-working and dedicated associates produced sales and profits that were the second-highest of any operating unit in the 23-year history of their company. He attributes his career to being at the right place at the right time, having the support of great associates, and being led by leaders willing to take a chance on regular folks—just like him.

Today, Russ and his wife, Sue, live in Bentonville, Arkansas. In addition to traveling and spending time with family and friends in the great outdoors, he enjoys corporate speaking and assisting executives and entrepreneurs in the area of developing leaders with the competence to generate a highly productive yet enjoyable work atmosphere.